MountainVision

Lessons From Beyond The Summit

Jeff Evans

First Printing 2007

Book design by Alex LaFasto
Cover photo by Didrik Johnck
www.johnck.com

ISBN 978-1-4276-2199-3

ATTENTION CORPORATIONS, UNIVERSITIES, COLLEGES AND PROFESSIONAL ORGANIZATIONS: Quantity discounts are available on bulk purchases of this book. Special books or book excerpts can also be created to fit special needs. For information, please contact MountainVision, 1024 55th Street, Boulder, CO 80303.

To all who seek
out adventure and
find meaning within it.

Acknowledgements

Throughout all of my adventures I have had a wonderful support group that has roped up with me in every sense of the word... time and time again and I am forever grateful to have these people in my life.

My grandparents, primarily my two grandfathers Pop and Bish, who instilled in me so much of the balance and determination required to be successful and safe in the mountains...even without knowing it.

My parents Bob and Peggy who have supported me in countless ways in spite of all of my best efforts to worry them (they would have much preferred I would have taken up golf). They have nurtured me and loved me as I have undoubtedly caused them much trouble and concern. I am forever indebted to them for all of their support.

My friends and climbing partners, primarily Erik, Chris and Gavin, who have been my brothers through thick and thin, have bled, suffered and cried in joy with me on the sides of mountains as well as on random barstools.

Matt and Alex, for helping me to get the words and the look right.

And finally and most profoundly to my wife Merry Beth and my son Jace who have provided me with the love and strength to continue on with my pursuits. They have taught me that all that matters in life exists within our family.

Never Let Go

Clinging desperately to the cascading wall of ice in front of me, I finally realize what the end looks like. I'm going to fall, and that will be that. My entire face goes numb and my heart screams as the rest of my body catches up with my inner ear. A moment ago I was clawing my way up this frozen tower. A split second later, one of my footholds has broken and I'm half a mile up and slowly sliding backwards. A million thoughts are trying to jam their way into the front of my mind, every one of them looking for a way out—any way out. My hands are in a frenzy, scratching with my ice picks against the slick surface in a losing fight. My boots can find no purchase below me, but I can't stop my legs from flailing wildly. The ice itself has warped my fingers into a frozen ache, but my face is burning white hot from the sun reflecting off it like a mirror. The pain is intense and searing, but I can't stop fighting because I'm running out of time.

More than the hurt, I'm aware of how this will end if I don't find a hold quickly. Thousands of feet above a pit of rocks, hundreds of miles from the nearest hospital, there isn't a lot of doubt about what my fate would be. I can see a dozen yards below me before the drop that will send me to my death. Trees and bushes look like small dots from the distance, but I'm aware of the jagged stones that surround them.

This is almost cliché, so many climbers I know have gone just like this… Fifteen feet now, still sliding. *Why didn't I stay home?* Twelve feet. *I don't want to die.* Now ten. *I wish I'd called my mother.* Five feet and I'm picking up speed now. *I wonder who will find my body?* My feet are the first to be freed of ground, swinging in the open air below them. I think of my family and hope they'll be alright.

And then, in that moment, I close my eyes and cringe. I hold my breath and wait, but the end doesn't come. Instead, I slowly open my eyes and realize that I'm stuck on something. I'm lying face down on an icy ridge, my hands bruised to the bone and my face burnt and blinded, but I'm breathing and not falling. There's nothing to do but smile and try to figure how long it will take me to get back up to where I was before I slipped.

Most people wonder from time to time how death will find them. For climbers this isn't just a morbid curiosity. Crawling up rocks and ice is one of those hobbies that provides you with plenty of opportunities to get whacked. I've got seconds to live, and a thought jumps into my head: *how does a guy who failed racquetball end up here?* I blame the ice cream man.

I'm asked again and again how I got started in climbing. It's tough to say how anyone truly gets into something like this, but I think it began when I was young. People like to imagine that I was the illegitimate child of a famous mountaineer and was raised by Sherpas. They wonder if I learned to walk on the icy slopes of Nepalese ranges, or maybe made my first ascents in the Alps while I was learning to read. These would make better stories, but the truth is I grew up near the Blue Ridge Mountains in Virginia. If you were to look on a map or a globe, you'd notice they're the kinds of mountains that are marked with green, not white. Which is to say, they aren't very high. Most people think of my neck of the woods as a place where moonshine comes from, not adventurers.

Nor were my parents the globe-trotting thrill seekers you might imagine. Neither one of them has climbed anything higher than a ladder, much less a large mass of ice and rock. My mom would really have preferred me to take up chess or golf, and it would have made sense. Besides living about as far as you can from any major mountain ranges, I wasn't a standout physical specimen. I was deemed too small to play basketball, too weak to play football, and too slow to run track.

Even with all these strikes against me, I think it's only inevitable that I found my way into this lifestyle. Because even though I wasn't fast or strong, even though I didn't come from the right place and wasn't the descendent of a long line of adventurers, I always wanted to see more. I was always a *seeker*.

The great thing about being young is that it doesn't matter if you're too small or too slow. You don't know enough about life to be bothered by limitations. For a kid, an adventure might be as far away as the front yard. And that's where the ice cream man comes in.

You see, when I was a small boy, maybe ten years old, the ice cream man was a magical and powerful figure. With a white truck literally filled with ice cream, he was something of a minor deity in my eyes. He was also, however, a very fast driver.

One of my favorite pastimes was to camp out in an old tree that grew in our yard. It had the kind of long, thick branches that just seemed to beg to be climbed. When school was out, I would spend those hot summer days scrambling from one wooden step to the next. For an imaginative kid, it was perfect. I would take in the breeze while sitting amongst the leaves, dreaming of far away places. Those branches gave me a love of climbing and exploring that's never faded.

Practically the only thing that would get me out of that tree was the sound of the ice cream man coming. By the time I heard the jingle-jangle music of his truck, I knew I only had a few seconds to get down and stop him before he passed my block and sped on to the next neighborhood. If I were too slow, it meant going without ice cream. With so much at stake, I developed a habit of maneuvering down the tree recklessly and then sprinting out to the street. Every day, the truck's melody would reach my ears and I'd fly into action, my hands and feet knowing exactly where to go. I always took it for granted that the branches would hold me. And then the branches, like so many things we take for granted, let me down.

I was working my way down at the usual break-neck pace on a particularly hot afternoon, when one of the tree's small arms snapped beneath me. My hands held on above, but both feet had given way and were dangling. I found myself hanging high above the ground. I was too young to figure how far down I would fall, but familiar enough with casts and crutches to know I needed to hold off gravity.

It was the first time that I can remember feeling like I'd worked myself into a spot I couldn't get out of. I struggled to think clearly, fighting back tears as the callous bark dug into my hands. It was frightening, but also exhilarating. At that moment, I was forced to learn an important lesson. When you're stuck – in a tree, on a rock, or in life – you basically have two choices: fall, or find a way down.

With my fingers bleeding and my shoulders burning, I realized falling was not an option. I started to edge myself from side to side, trying to reach another branch. Each movement seemed to bring a fresh wave of sharp pain. Every piece of me begged to let go, but none more than my hands. They stung, spilling fresh blood as I inched myself along the rough bark. Finally, through short breaths and choked tears, I swung my left hand toward a smoother branch that offered a relief. If I could reach it, I'd make it to safety, but if I missed, I'd be in for a nasty spill. Luckily, I was able to get to it just in time, and after a couple of painful minutes, I was back down on the ground. The ice cream man was gone, but I had discovered a passion and a strength that would help me for the rest of my life.

That situation has played itself out for me hundreds of times on rocks and ice around the world. The scenery has changed, I'm no longer in my favorite tree, instead I'm usually facing an unfriendly wall of rock and ice. But the premise is the same: hang on or die.

Though sometimes it's cut a bit closer than I'd like it to be, I've survived in this profession not by being the biggest or fastest, but by choosing not to fall. You can choose to hang on, too. Remember, I'm just a kid who wanted some ice cream. Who were you?

Stumbling to Enlightenment

Even though I had found some inner strength, I still lacked discipline. Like a lot of kids with no direction, I did just enough to get by. I was that student who was always looking to squeak through with a barely passing grade. Outside the classroom I was getting into small kinds of trouble that landed me on the inside of a jail cell a couple of times. It was never anything serious, but anyone could see that I was just drifting through life without making a real effort.

Still, I made my way to college at East Tennessee State, where I proceeded to set new lows for academic achievement. I was probably doomed from the start. When it came time to choose a major, I drew a blank. Part of me was drawn to medicine. As a child, my favorite toy had been a play medical kit that I'd gotten for my fifth birthday. For years, I carried it around with me, diagnosing friends and relatives, sometimes 'curing' them with the plastic stethoscope and hammer. Since then, working with medicine had been a dream of mine. But when I got to the university, I found out that my bad grades, along with the long years needed to earn an MD, would almost certainly keep me away from ever achieving that dream.

With no other promising options, I decided on business. After all, wasn't that what most people studied? And besides, almost everyone works in one business or another, so I figured it would set me on the right path. Unfortunately, it didn't work out that way.

I spent my days hanging out with my friends and generally not showing up for classes. After earning a stellar 1.25 GPA in my first semester, I was allowed back to school under academic probation for a second try. I'd love to say that I'd learned my lesson and buckled down to graduate with honors.

In reality, I outdid my first effort by earning a 0.6 in my second semester. If your memory of the college grading scale is rusty, keep in mind that you earn four points for an 'A,' three for a 'B' and two for a 'C.' They even give you a point for a 'D.' So, to receive a cumulative grade of 0.6, you pretty much have to get a single D somewhere and then a bunch of 'F's. I didn't even pass racquetball. In most states that doesn't only disqualify you from college, but also from being tried as an adult.

While my mental capabilities didn't classify me as handicapped, the truth is that my motivation at that point probably could have. On the rare occasion that I'd actually go to class, I'd sleep through it and then go out drinking or hiking with my buddies. I just didn't understand what people wanted with school, or why they should bother to pay attention. These days, I would have probably been given a prescription for some kind of calming medicine, but all I could do then was find an outlet for my energy. And in climbing, I did. Just as that old tree had been my refuge when I was a small boy, the rock growths and wilderness areas near campus became a place for me to get away from the settings where I didn't fit in.

I didn't have any patience for Biology or English, where everything seemed so abstract and dull. The more you read, the more questions you had. The more questions you had, the more classes you had to take. In the classroom, there was never any action, only more words to go round and round with, which never led to any solid conclusions. On the side of a rocky hill, things were clear. All you had to do was concentrate and keep going up. Sooner or later, you'd reach the top.

After my grades came in for the second term, continuing college was out of the question. With no sense of purpose, I decided it was time to go out and see something new. I wanted to get away from what I had already experienced and try my luck somewhere different. With two hundred and fifty dollars in my pocket, I decided to go where anyone who had a passion for climbing would - Colorado. I expected a stiff lecture from my parents, but to their credit, they didn't try to keep me from it. I think they realized that sending me back to school was pointless. Besides, after being out in the world for a couple of months, maybe I'd come home. Broke and hungry, sure, but also ready to buckle down and grow up. What they didn't realize was that I wasn't interested in money or a good job. I wanted to find something that would pull me out of bed each morning and bring some adventure to my life.

The drive out west was long, but I loved every minute of it. As the green hills in the southeast gave way to the wide open plains across Kansas and Oklahoma, my mind raced with the new possibilities in front of me. Farther in, I could see the mountains towering in the distance, like heavy thunderclouds all the way up into the sky. Once I reached the Rockies, I was in love. These were the kinds of rugged hills I'd always dreamed of, places where you could explore for weeks and never find yourself on the same trail.

When I stopped driving, I found myself in a small, Colorado mountain town, working odd jobs as a dishwasher or bellboy to keep myself barely fed. The rest of the time, I poured myself into climbing. Every day was a chance to explore a new rock or meet a new summit. My hair grew long and my fingers scraped every day until they bled, but it made my climbing mind sharp. I kept this up for a couple of years, until I decided I needed some new scenery and headed West to Joshua Tree in California.

If you aren't a climber, Joshua Tree is probably what you'd think of as kind of a wasteland. A couple hours east of Los Angeles, it's basically a desert with some really crazy rock structures jutting from the earth. Inside the park, formations fill the landscape for as far as the eye can see in any direction. Some are small, only twenty or thirty feet up on a side. Others are larger, like apartment buildings, with walls that move and shift at extreme angles.

By the time I got there, I was what mountaineering enthusiasts might call a rock rat, or what normal people call a dirt bag. I'd taken poverty and lack of motivation to a whole new level. While I'd been living in basements for a few dollars a week in Colorado, I decided to give up those luxuries so I wouldn't have to hold a job. I didn't have any steady income, but I was completely unencumbered. I still needed a few dollars here and there to get by, but otherwise I was free to do whatever I wanted. Sleeping in the back of a pickup truck without regular gainful employment isn't what most folks consider a worthy endeavor, but for me it was the best thing in the world. I spent my days doing the only thing I cared about – climbing. Anything else, whether scrounging for food or taking the occasional day job to buy new gear, was aimed at getting me back to climbing.

Some kids go to college, some go straight to the military or the workforce; a few even backpack around Europe for a while. Not me. I decided to give the homeless route a try. And while nearly everyone would consider this a waste of time, it was the best thing that could have happened to me. I was finally free of the hopes and expectations everyone else had for me. In that space, I was able to discover what motivation and focus were really about. Instead of doing things for other people, or because I was supposed to, I started thinking about them for myself. I didn't want to be a lawyer or an accountant, but I probably wouldn't want to live outside forever. I finally started taking a look at my future and realizing I could follow things that would make me happy, not that I was sure what that meant.

I certainly hadn't given much thought to going back to school, though it wasn't that I was completely against the idea. It was more that I still didn't see how it could take me anywhere I wanted to go. The rest of the world might think college was a good idea, but I'd been there and done that. Still, you can only escape the rest of the world for so long.

There were a lot of parties in Joshua Tree, but they weren't formal, catered affairs. Usually it was the case that someone from the 'community' scraped up a few dollars for some pizza and beer, along with whatever else they might be growing in the desert. Everyone crawled out of their vans, tents, or trucks and got together to celebrate being dirt bag hippies. These get-togethers were a great time, but it didn't lead to a lot of interaction with the outside world. I grew to sometimes miss things like clean towels, food that didn't come in bar form, and especially, girls who didn't smell like they'd been climbing in the desert heat for three weeks straight. And so, when one of my friends invited me to a party outside the park, I jumped at the chance. And there, I met a girl who would change my life.

To write in a book that a chance meeting with a pretty girl changed your life is a bit cliché, but it's true nonetheless. What's unusual about my story is that this girl didn't end up being a significant figure in my life. It was only one moment, a brief conversation, that changed my course. I was having a great time that evening, taking in the fresh smells and sites, when I saw her. She caught my eye right away, pulling me out of whatever thoughts were swimming in my head. She was tall and beautiful, but it wasn't her physical attractiveness that struck me right away. It was the way she seemed to radiate confidence and poise. Even from a distance, I could see she spoke evenly, with a measured tone. She thought for a moment before she spoke, and everyone seemed to listen. Not only because she was stunning, but because she had interesting thoughts and ideas.

Approaching her wouldn't be easy. To say that she was somewhat outside my normal circle of friends is a bit of an understatement. I looked and smelled like a refugee; every detail of her appearance seemed to suggest a kind of purpose and precision. Even though I was no match, I knew I had to try. I walked over and gave my best opening pitch, trying to gently work my way into the conversation at hand.

Probably sensing my interest, or possibly my lack of deodorant, her friends peeled away from us one by one. I kept the conversation moving with questions about her life: where she was from, what she liked to do, how I could also pretend to know and like those things. Talking with her was fascinating and intimidating. I found out she was a student at Brown University, in the Ivy League, and nearing her graduation. She had been places I hadn't seen, read books I'd never heard of, and quoted people whose names I couldn't pronounce. By the end of the evening, I had figured out two things: she wasn't interested in coming back to my sleeping bag in the park, and that I wanted to be smarter, too. Talking with her had made me aware of how many things I was ignorant of, and how I was never going to be able to get over that without going back to school.

This realization brought its own problems. The road to college is considerably more difficult when you're no longer a student. It had been years since I'd picked up a book, and even then, I'd never taken my education seriously. With my poor track record, what college would accept me? And besides, what would I study even if I got in? I had been so bored taking business classes, the thought of it made me want to throw myself off the nearest cliff.

I spent the next few days thinking these things over. I knew I couldn't study business, it just wasn't in me, but I didn't know what else I could try. The only thing that held my attention, besides medicine, was learning about different people around the world. If only there was some way to study foreign cultures, instead of things like accounting. That's when it hit me like a two ton artifact – cultural anthropology.

For the first time, I would use my interests to learn and move forward, instead of shirking my motivation. To make it happen, I knew I needed to get out of Joshua Tree and back on sturdier footing. I continued living in my truck to save money, but I took a small part-time job at a local climbing gear outfitter, storing away my tiny paychecks until I could move into a real place again.

After a few months, I'd saved enough and decided I would go back to Colorado. I was able to rent a mobile home in a small alpine village for next to nothing and use the rest of my money to take some correspondence classes. When I came to "previous college" on the application, I simply checked 'none.' As the weeks went by, I devoured the lessons that arrived by mail. Week after week I worked with books, quizzes and papers, flying through one course and then another. I found I actually loved learning, regretting the years I'd spent away from it. All the while I was terrified the university might find out about my previous stint and revoke my admission, but the expulsion never came.

I buried myself in my studies as I'd done with climbing before, but I didn't want to give up my love of the outdoors. My parents, wanting to help me make something of myself, pitched in, but I could no longer afford to skip work and go out every day if I wanted to keep paying my rent and tuition. The decision to almost completely give up my one true love for another pursuit was heart-wrenching for me. I worked in kitchens or hotels, taking small jobs in the industries that spring up around ski towns. I'd stumble through my duties, wishing I were in the hills climbing, instead of scraping food from dishes or carrying luggage. On my few spare days off from work and studying, I'd head to a local rock face and climb from dawn to dusk.

This might have gone on for months or years if I hadn't run into some new climbers one morning. The sun was just breaking out, and I wanted to get up the rock wall I was working on one more time before I had to shuttle off to work. The group saw me climbing from below and was impressed by the comfort I showed while moving across the face. New to the sport, they would slowly amble their way towards the top, double checking each hold, tentatively working with their ropes and gear. For someone like me who had gone through years of daily climbing, the section was nearly effortless. Just as an experienced ballplayer might step out to the batting cages to relieve stress, I was on this pitch for the relaxation, not the challenge. Noticing the vast difference in our skill, one of them approached me about an impromptu lesson. I told them I'd love to help out, but that I needed to get back to work to pay the rent. "Maybe some other time," I told them. And then, I reached another pivotal moment in my life. A member of the group offered to pay me for my time.

I had heard of guiding for money, but never thought it was something I could do. I didn't work for any big company or have any special training. I was just a climbing bum who had learned some things. I didn't consider myself to be any kind of expert, but that didn't matter. What I learned that day was if you have a lot more knowledge and experience on a topic than someone else, to that person you're an expert. You can help them get to where they want to go, even if you're still working out your own challenges on a different level. This turned out to be a revelation in my life, and one that's taken me far.

In the following weeks I took on more and more guiding

clients. I didn't want to work for a big company or wear a tie, and it gave me a way to be out in the mountains when I wasn't studying. I made a point of being out where other climbers would be around. Newer climbers would see me scaling the rocks and ask if I'd take them up or show them some tips. So, I started charging a few dollars for an on-the-spot lesson. Soon, I was giving longer lessons, and then overnight trips on actual mountains. Eventually, I was able to quit the other odd jobs I worked. It was barely enough money to pay the bills, but it did put cash in my pocket, and more importantly, it taught me to be responsible for other people. In the end, that new sense of responsibility made the rest of my life, and the stories that make up the rest of this book, possible.

The Diamond That Didn't Shine

The Diamond is a 1,500 foot glistening rock face on the east side of Long's Peak, in Rocky Mountain National Park. To me, every mountain is a magical place, but the Diamond especially so. With a granite face infused with composite metals, it gleams red, green, yellow, and black, as if God cut a perfectly sharpened flat surface into the side of an already beautiful mountain and left the exposed jewels to shine in the sun. Besides its natural beauty, climbers love the Diamond because it offers a unique technical challenge. Its face extends more than five-hundred yards at a magnificent angle, making it more like scaling the Sears tower than the side of a mountain.

All of this came to mind when a friend, Lou, asked me if I'd be interested in taking a crack at it. Lou was a lot like me at the time, except maybe that he had dirt bag seniority. I was still fairly new to climbing, living in a basement somewhere and washing dishes a couple times a week to earn the small amount of money I needed for gear and meals. Lou had taken this philosophy even further, forgoing the basement and menial labor. Some people might have thought twice about looking up to a homeless person as a role model, but he had been climbing a year or so longer than I had so, in my eyes, he was a hero.

Besides, I was eager to give the Diamond a go, and was a bit embarrassed not to have tried it before. It was, as I remember reading once, 'something any serious mountaineer must attempt.' I *knew* I was serious, and this one was in my back yard. Thinking of the climb itself left a pit in my stomach, but I could no longer bear to hear my friends talk about their adventures on the face. While he didn't say so, I'm sure Lou felt the same way. Neither of us had so much as hiked up to the base before. Our pride was on the line, and we were going to go and set things right.

A three-hour hike took us through an alpine trail dotted with robust pines and sun soaked aspens that led to the area where we would begin our ascent in earnest. Breaking through the last section of dense forest, we were deposited into the valley where we'd get our first look at the Diamond up close. It's hard to describe what I felt, but I could tell my stomach was already against the idea. The immediate stabbing pain in my gut was accompanied by a lightheaded sensation. My pulse jumped and my mouth numbed. Put another way, I was terrified. This was not going to be as easy as I'd imagined. Staring up at the steep face, the words *bad idea* came to mind again and again. I glanced over at Lou. He wore the thin, forced smile of a man overcome with dread. He turned to face me, and we shared an uncomfortable moment where neither of us could find the words to rescue ourselves from our conundrum.

We had come to salvage our pride, and neither of us wanted to be the one to back down. We were in way over our heads, and we both knew it, but our self-respect wasn't going to allow us to save ourselves. We didn't find much conversation as we set up camp for a short night of listless sleep, neither of us speaking about the elephant in the room. We didn't have to – it was staring us down from a hundred yards away.

Throughout the short night I had writhed listlessly in my

sleeping bag, and could hear Lou doing the same. As the hours wore on, I cursed the calm weather. I wished for a spot of wind or rain, anything to cover the silence of our sleeplessness, interrupted only by our tossing and turning. Our fear of what to come was making us writhe and squirm like children in a dentist's waiting room. When the alarm went off at 3 a.m., I was relieved.

We gathered our gear by the moonlight, double and triple-checking each piece in our collection. I stayed quiet, afraid that my voice would betray me and crack with fear. Finally, there was nothing to do but begin.

Lou took the first *pitch*, a section of vertical climbing one rope-length long, about two-hundred feet. We roped into each other and our gear, taking special care with the knots we were relying upon to save us if we fell. Then, Lou made his first reaches upward. He went slowly, each movement tentative, a stark contrast to the brisk pace we were used to making together. I led the next section, following Lou's deliberate, hesitant example. We continued on, one pitch after another, trying not to look down at the earth slowly sinking below us, or the more menacing areas still waiting above. The hours passed and we crawled our way a bit further up, one rope length at a time. These approach pitches took us through to the base of the route, setting us up for the challenge ahead. Finally, near day break, we had come to the section of the Diamond that set it apart – the vertical cliff that extends upward for hundreds of feet.

As dangerous and awe-inspiring as the geometry of the face is, the truly terrifying thing about the Diamond is that it's on the East side. That would be a trivial fact, except weather typically comes in from the West, hidden by the mountain itself. The side of a mountain, or a rock face, is the last place you want to be when a storm moves in. Wind, snow, hail, and lightning are all extremely dangerous at altitude. Worst of all, high alpine conditions can change very rapidly, sometimes in minutes. Like an alcoholic uncle, these storms can show up at any time, but tend to avoid the mornings. Afternoons tend to be particularly treacherous; the sun has had time to heat up the earth, throw some moisture in the air and start causing trouble. That's why most climbers start out for the summit in the middle of the night or early morning hours. To summit at dawn isn't only beautiful, it could also save your life.

We had gotten an early start, but were progressing slowly. The sun had crawled over the horizon hours before, and we were only now ready to begin the more demanding work ahead. The forecast had been clear, and I knew we were fortunate for the calm winds and bright morning. However, as we paused for a momentary rest, I looked up and noticed the faintest shred of white moving in over the summit, directly above us. It didn't look to be so much a cloud as it did a spray of mist in the air, but I pointed it out to Lou. He took it in with a look of deep concern as both of us stared, unspeaking, at the minute whisper of water floating by above us. As much of a concern as weather is on a mountain, we knew it was nothing. Nonetheless, it was an excuse that could get us out of a place we didn't want to be. I didn't want to appear too eager to give up. We sat in an awkward hush for several moments.

Finally, Lou broke the silence. "Well, what do you think?"

"Hmm," I answered, pretending to think on it deeply. I frowned and shook my head a bit. "Could get nasty. We don't want to get caught up here in that. Might not be safe." And then the clincher, "I couldn't live with myself if I pushed this and something happened to you."

Lou paused, as if greatly pained. "It doesn't look like much," he nearly whispered. *What? How could he say that?* I was struck again with fear. He was holding too tightly to his dignity, and if he kept it up, we just might have to climb this thing. Luckily, whatever part of my brain generates excuses went into overdrive.

"I think I see some gray," I volunteered. *Gray?* Had I really just said that?

"Well, perhaps we should call it a day and give it a try some other time." He tried to sound sorry, but the relief in his voice was palpable. I played along, adding that we'd made a good run at it, but the conditions just weren't right. The conversation continued on and on as we sped our way down to the base. *We'd love to finish this,* we told ourselves and each other, *but the weather!*

Two hours later, after we'd reached the safety of flat ground in record time, Lou and I admired the perfectly clear crystal-blue sky. We patted ourselves on the back for being such careful climbers, and for being so concerned with each other's safety. Of course, we each knew we were lying. The truth was, we were out of our league, and so stricken with fear we could barely move. There's nothing wrong with that, but, we were also both too proud to admit it, which had forced us into a bad situation and left us feeling worse.

Months later, after we'd both had a good deal more practice and preparation, we went back to the Diamond and climbed it successfully. We knew what we were doing and didn't have to invent excuses for our lack of progress. The ascent itself was pretty unremarkable. The route was even tougher than we'd imagined at the top, but this time we were ready for the challenge. The sensation of completing a tough climb was good. Beating back my fears was even better.

Retreat is not surrender. If you find yourself in over your head, it's better to face up to that and come back when you're ready. The first time I'd gone to the Diamond I was looking for a way out. The second time, I was looking for a way to get it done.

Learning to Lead

After completing a few correspondence classes, I moved on to a full-time program at the University of Colorado. There, I spent the next three years trying to make my way through it by keeping up a schedule that would allow me to make academic progress, live indoors, and keep climbing. I would sign up for early classes so that I could attend in the morning, guide climbers in hills near campus during the afternoon, and then shuttle back home to study.

It was a great life, and it gave me a good outlet for all of my energy and ambition. Just as I'd learned I could enjoy my education, I came to discover I'd actually come to appreciate guiding as well. What I had begun pursuing for the money was turning out to give me deeper fulfillment. There was something amazing about working with my clients to make them stronger, better climbers. Many of them became interested in climbing because they had seen others scaling rocks and wanted to try the sport themselves. Often, however, they lacked the confidence that they would be able to learn, and would start out afraid and doubting themselves. Hour by hour, as their technical skills improved, I watched their hesitation melt away. Seeing the sense of accomplishment in their faces and watching fear turn into strength became worth more than the few dollars that were exchanged.

What's more, that fulfillment carried over into my coursework. My grades were better than they had ever been, even after I began taking extra classes to finish my degree more quickly. My only real question was what to do after graduation. I loved my studies in anthropology, but I couldn't find anything in the field that would keep me outdoors, and I knew I wouldn't function in an office environment. Luckily, the answer found me.

I woke up early one Saturday morning, reveling in the freedom and possibilities held by a morning without classes or clients. I decided to head to the outskirts of town to scale the Boulder Flatirons. The Flatirons are a set of massive stone walls that jump out at you from miles away. The array of jagged faces, all of them nearly vertical, make the small mountain that they sit upon look as if it had been carved open on its side. Like the Diamond, they have a geometry that makes them beautiful to hikers and irresistible to climbers. They were also convenient, requiring only a short drive and a few hours to complete.

I had scaled the Flatirons dozens, if not hundreds of times, so I let my thoughts wander as I set out on the short trail that led to the first pitch. While my mind wrestled with all of my worries about the future, turning the possibilities over and over, I tread through the high grass and rough thickets that come to the Colorado backcountry in spring. I was so lost in my own thoughts, it wasn't until I found myself a few yards away that I noticed the pieces of gear glinting and reflecting just off the gravel path. I leaned over for a closer look, examining small shards of shiny metal and bright fabric strewn across the green and brown surface. Slowly, I edged my way into the brush, already sure and afraid of what I would find. A few more steps revealed more scraps, and a large impression in the earth no more than three yards further. I couldn't see into the bushes that had been smothered and depressed, but there was no longer any doubt. Bears didn't wear bright orange. Finally, I reached my hand out to clear away the small twigs blocking my view and gazed upon the fallen climber.

I prayed silently he would be alive and well, but he wasn't making a sound. It was possible, I reasoned, that he might just be injured. Either way, I didn't know what to do. I studied him for a moment, limp and unmoving, and then began to yell for help. My voice carried through to the trail, and soon half a dozen others had joined me, all of us screaming out for someone who could help. I could finally make out short breaths, but still wasn't sure how to help. The only thing that came to mind was to keep clamoring, and so I did. After a few minutes of this, a man came rushing down the path and pushed us aside to reach the fallen climber. He moved in toward the body quickly, but with precision. He placed a finger to check the man's pulse and lowered his ear to listen for breathing. His hands moved with practiced skill, in opposition to the panic around him. He began to check for breaks and bruises, and then spent time reviving his patient. Finally, he rose and stepped away from the climber and informed us the young man would be alright. He'd shattered an ankle and had the wind knocked out of him, but the injuries were much less serious than they could have been.

In that moment, my mind was flooded by all those dreams of medicine going all the way back to my childhood. The thought of so many years of school still seemed overwhelming, but I wanted to be a doctor just like this man. I overcame my shock of the last few minutes to walk with him as the injured younger man was carried to get medical attention. I wanted to find out where he worked, where he'd gone to medical school, and how I could learn the skills he had. His expression was one of slight surprise and amusement. "Oh, I'm not a doctor," he explained.

"I'm an EMT."

I went straight home to find whatever I could about Emergency Medical Technicians. I found out that EMT's were often the first line of medical care, especially in the backcountry. There was even a unique kind of tech, the Wilderness EMT, who specialized in situations like the one I'd seen. Courses were three months long, and taught in Colorado. I began to think and conjure up ways to afford the tuition. The course began just days after my graduation, and there wouldn't be much time to save. I couldn't find a way, but my mind wouldn't let it go. I had finally found a track that would allow me to combine my love of medicine and my love of mountains. I couldn't bear the thought of not going.

As luck would have it, the perfect opportunity arrived. My parents, proud and relieved that I'd given up homelessness to work my way to a college degree, wanted to get me something special for graduation. They asked what it was that I was dying to have. Was it a car, a new computer, maybe a vacation abroad? I think they were stunned by my answer — tuition for another course. Like a five-year-old in the supermarket check-out line with a small toy in hand, I proceeded to list off all of wonderful benefits I could get from the program, and how it actually wasn't that expensive at all if you really thought about it. It was an investment in my future, and I'd certainly learn skills that would carry over to a lucrative position. On and on I went, until they finally stopped me mid-sentence. They would cover my tuition. They were just happy I didn't ask for a holiday in Amsterdam.

The wilderness EMT course was a blast. In addition to learning about basic life support, wound care and other forms of medical treatment and the ins and outs of backcountry medical emergencies, I made close friends. I suddenly found myself in a community of men and women who understood me. The kind of people who sign up for a course like this do so because they want to help others, but also because they love those wild places. They could relate to the restlessness I felt in the classroom or an office. Like me, they'd decided they wanted lives filled with adventure, but not without the occasional shower or hot meal. The weeks went by like a dream. Mornings were filled with practical, hands-on medical training, usually outdoors. Our afternoons were free for climbing, kayaking and talking about the techniques we'd learned that day.

It was during the first week of class that I met Sam, a fellow climber and student. He was in his twenties, just like I was, and also looking for a way to make more out of his love for the backcountry. He was newer to climbing but shared my love of adventure. He would try anything. He'd been skydiving, windsurfing, and hiking through some of the most rugged terrain in the state. He was new to technical climbing, but was absorbing it passionately and with the same abandon. He took in new rocks and hills every week, going up with anyone who was interested. In his hometown of Phoenix, he had even gone climbing with a friend of his who was blind. I couldn't imagine such a thing, although he had invited me along a couple of times. Sam and I hit it off right away, and would often spend time studying or climbing together. One Friday morning, just after classes, he asked if I'd be interested in taking in a longer technical climb over the weekend. With no plans in place, it seemed like a great idea.

We decided we would climb Lizard Head, a moderately difficult hunk of jagged stone cut out from the earth deep in the San Juan range of the Rocky Mountains. While not as high or technically challenging as many climbs in the Rockies, Lizard Head can be tough because it wears you down. Just to reach the base of the rock from the trailhead takes a hike lasting about a day. Then, when you set up for your actual ascent, the climb itself could take over eight hours. You only scale about eight-hundred vertical feet, but it twists and bends around craggy features with its base at twelve-thousand feet. Plus, the lack of oxygen at that starting altitude makes the ascent physically demanding. Add the unpredictable weather and the remote location, and you've got a tough haul with very little chance for help if you need it.

The approach climb was long and grueling, the path leading to the face marked by worn trails that had often turned to scree, piles of small pebbles that easily gave way under foot. Relishing the challenge, we kept a steady pace on a path that crept first through a dense, forested corridor and then twisted and turned into nothing more than ashen gray rocks above tree line. There was no way through except to keep putting one foot after another, which we did until the vertical rope climb leading to the top was in sight. Here, we setup camp for the evening. Sam and I settled in, eager to go the rest of the way.

We didn't have to wait too long. In the early hours of the morning, our alarm went off and we set out towards the top. For several hours, we clawed our way up, inch by inch, conquering each of the thousand feet in small sips of breath and pain. We finally reached the summit, exhausted, but pleased to have made it. We sat together, taking in the silence and peace of the moment. I crouched on the ground and lay back to catch my breath and take in the afternoon sun. Sam pulled out his camera to snap a few photos, thus being the first one to spot the nasty weather brewing on the horizon. The ability to tell the difference between good or bad weather in the mountains can be a bit of a guessing game, as mountain clouds are notoriously ambiguous, but this wasn't one of those times. The puffy, gray clouds approaching the summit were unmistakable. In our enjoyment of a hard route, we hadn't noticed the day was reaching late into the afternoon - prime time for mountain storms. In other words, we had reached the summit just in time for the meteorological equivalent of rush hour traffic.

Our satisfaction melted into fear as we started to calculate the time it would take us to get down against the number of precious minutes left before the weather would arrive. Our only option was to hurry back down the rocky tower we'd just spent hours pulling ourselves up, exhausted from the climb and lack of rest afterward. Without spending any more of the usual time at a summit to enjoy the moment and take in the views, we started down. Moving quickly but not recklessly, we hoped the thunder we could hear in the distance would hold off just long enough. After about twenty minutes of frenzied movement, dodging sharp edges with tired legs and bleary eyes, we realized that we weren't going to reach the safety of camp in time. Perched on a small, flat stone, I sat down with my legs folded to my chest to keep them from dangling over the side of a cliff that went down at least seven stories. We were in the thick of it, the sky rumbling above us, another three or four rope-lengths of descent laying below, and there was no easy way out.

I wasn't sure which way to go – the descent would be dangerous, but trying to wait out the storm on a too-small ledge might kill us. When you're loaded down with climbing gear, thousands of pieces of jangling metal, a thunderstorm is not the place you want to find yourself. The wind was picking up, small pebbles stung my eyes, and I knew we couldn't stay long. A loud clap of thunder came with a flash not far enough away, and the hairs on the back of my neck told me they understood the trouble. My nerves were starting to eat me alive, but just like when I was a child, I realized we had a choice: we could either lose our cool and almost certainly lose our lives, or stay calm and keep working toward the bottom. I decided that if I was going to die, I'd rather have it be on the way down.

Sam had apparently arrived at the same conclusion but seemed to be dealing with it differently. As the seriousness of our trouble set in, he started talking more quickly and desperately.

"I don't want to get pasted here," he murmured. I told him we should try to make our way down a bit further. We took a glance over the ledge where we would use our gear and ropes to try a descent, when I realized he was on the edge of losing his head.

Fear is a natural emotion, and it has its place in any adventure. After all, without the sense of fear and risk, climbs would become nature walks and wouldn't carry the excitement they do. But Sam's fear had overcome him. He was becoming unhinged, and it was making the situation even more dangerous than it already was. As my climbing experience gave me a keen awareness of how dire things were, I was probably more afraid than he was. Nonetheless, I knew we needed to manage it and move on if we were to have any hope of surviving.

So, in a gesture fit for Hollywood, I slapped him across the face and told him to pull it together. I explained that if we were going to be killed, better by a quick fall than waiting there to be blown off the cliff or struck by lightning. Sam didn't speak, but nodded his head in agreement, and we started to move down.

The rocks were smooth and worn, there was no where to grip or place any equipment. Our only option would be an old rappel that had been left in by a previous team. I didn't like the looks of it. The small anchor that would hold our weight was nothing more than a piton, a tiny tool that looked like a small spike, driven into some loose rock. As I inserted the rope, it flexed and gave way. I couldn't be sure if it would hold our weight, but we didn't have any other options.

I headed down on the first rappel. The wet rocks conspired with a biting wind to swing us from side to side as the anchor swiveled. I expected it to pop out at any moment, dropping us backward to the ground below. I felt petrified of the fall, but each time I came close to stopping, I would look up at the hard rain and lightning crashing up at the peak and find the courage to make my way a bit further down.

Of course, we eventually made it to the bottom with a few new scars and a story to tell. Sam had composed himself beautifully and actually went first on several of the rappels when I became too fatigued. Down at the base, he acknowledged he had lost his nerve for a moment and needed that slap to bring him back.

Moments like those aren't that uncommon between climbing buddies, and it wouldn't have been a big deal if he hadn't again mentioned his friend, Erik, the blind climber. He said after what we'd been through that day, he thought I should give working with him some more thought. Erik was a good friend, he told me, and someone who was ready to take his adventuring to the next level. But, he wouldn't be able to do it alone. Sam said there was no one else with whom he'd rather trust his friend and that we might make a good team. I told him I would think about it, and for the first time, I actually did.

I See the Light

When I first met Erik Weihenmayer, I was living in Joshua Tree again. After the years of hard work spent getting first my degree and then my wilderness EMT certification, I wanted to blow off some steam. The manager of a local gear company whom I'd kept in touch with had offered me a few hours for the remainder of the summer selling climbing equipment. It sounded like the perfect chance to regroup, and get back to my dirt bag climbing roots.

I bought an old pickup truck for the trip out and made it my home for those few months. Each week I worked a couple of shifts at the store so I could afford ramen noodles and the occasional beer. Mostly though, I woke up smelling like sweaty garbage and climbed all day until it was time to crawl back into my sleeping bag and wait for the next morning. Sometimes I didn't shower for weeks on end, and I was loving it. For all I'd accomplished, I came to realize that sometimes it feels good to just let go and live carefree. Some people save for vacations to Paris or Tahiti, I just wanted to get back to the desert for a break.

I had given some thought to what Sam said that day in Colorado, and decided I would give it a shot if Erik wanted to come on out to my 'home.' Sure enough, he said he'd love to. Besides seeing what kind of climbing chemistry we had, Joshua Tree would serve as a good barometer of his talents and abilities.

When Sam's car pulled up, I had my first look at his blind friend. Sam helped him from the car, while I watched on from the bed of my truck in disbelief. I couldn't imagine this guy could make it up the stairs, much less any natural upward-facing feature on earth. He looked a mess in every conceivable way. He was obviously athletic, but was so white that I wondered if he might have gone blind from living in a cave. His pale skin was accentuated by an outfit that made him appear to be a roadie for the world's most awkward metal band – a mullet, some tattered jeans, a t-shirt, and a denim jacket with an Iron Maiden patch on it. Worst of all, the different kinds of denim didn't even seem to go together. Neither did his socks. I wondered if there wasn't some sort of blind dressing the blind thing going on. *Wow*, I thought, *he's not just blind – he's colorblind!*

I was already disappointed, but after Sam introduced us, the ridiculousness of the situation became apparent. Here I was, essentially homeless, in the middle of desert and rocks with a blind man who wanted to climb with me—dog, stick and all. Erik either sensed my lack of enthusiasm, or was having doubts of his own. Even though I knew he couldn't see me, I tried to hide the skepticism from my face. The moment was heavy and awkward with no one volunteering anything to say. Finally, I mumbled that we might as well go up some rocks while the day was young. In truth, I thought it best to get this over with as quickly as possible. It seemed like my morning was about to be ruined, but I might still be able to get rid of him by afternoon. And so, with the help of his seeing-eye dog, I led Erik over to the first pitch.

The small community of dirt bags living in Joshua Tree were used to seeing a lot of things. Situations that might seem outrageous in the civilized world wouldn't cause them to look twice. This was a place that attracted people who wanted to live in trucks and vans and crawl around dusty rocks all day. Drunken fights, bad acid trips, and naked climbers were all pretty regular sights and sounds. Now I had something that topped them all. As my neighbors peered on curiously, I led the way for a man with a seeing-eye dog to the first pitch and roped him up. Jaws dropped. I could see men and women looking at one another and mouthing out, 'are you serious?' We were about to find out.

I started up the first pitch. It was a relatively easy climb, and one I'd done several times before. I moved from hold to hold quickly and smoothly, hoping to expedite Erik's departure back to wherever he came from. I couldn't remember what I'd been thinking when I agreed to this, but both lobes of my brain now considered it a mistake. Clearly, the thing to do was to get to the top and let him figure out that why there were no other blind climbers.

I reached the end of the short pitch quickly. Now it was Erik's turn. Without any sort of hesitation, he reached up to find the first hold, and then the second. He wasn't fast, but he wasn't sloppy either. He seemed to have a natural sense for positioning, and would slip easily from one spot to the next. Perhaps, I thought, I'd underestimated him. He might be able to enjoy himself on some of the easier sections while I kept an eye out. Before long, he had reached the top where I was waiting. I was impressed with his grit, and thought about taking him somewhere more challenging after he'd had a chance to rest and catch his breath. But before either of us could get comfortable, he turned my direction and asked, "What's next?" I couldn't help but smile.

Curious now, I led him down and onto a more difficult route, one longer and more technically challenging. Again he surprised me with his calm determination. While he didn't have the benefit of experience, he never got flustered and simply kept moving until he found his way. He was a very strong climber for a beginner, sighted or not. In fact, for him, getting up the pitches wasn't the hard part. Rather, it was in getting from one rock to the next. The park was crowded with people and gear, which Erik occasionally walked into or through.

He, of course, couldn't see anybody, and no one seemed to be looking out for him. Several times, as we made our way from one formation to another, he'd crash into another group of climbers. I tried to steer him with the help of his dog, but it was impossible to stop him from getting in the way. He never complained or said he was sorry, just made his way through until we were ready to start a new pitch. He seemed to understand that you just didn't expect to see a blind man in Joshua Tree climbing next to you, but he didn't apologize for it either.

Following each ascent I'd look at him, pale and mulleted in his mismatched clothes. I had worried he wouldn't have the stamina to make it up even one stone face. Instead, he took climb after climb, never slowing or asking for rest.

After a few hours, we became familiar enough for me to ask the questions that had been sitting on my mind all day. *Who was he and why was he doing this?*

Erik's dad was a former Marine. Like a lot of military children, he had grown up in different places all around the world. His early years in Shanghai, Korea, Europe and throughout the US had instilled in him a strong sense of adventure and curiosity. Even if he couldn't see, he always wanted to know what new things sounded like, smelled like and especially *felt* like.

He hadn't been born blind. As a child he had been diagnosed with retinoscheses, a degenerative eye disease that caused his retina to unravel over time. The condition was irreversible, and from a very early age he knew that he would eventually go completely blind. His sight continued to worsen, growing darker and darker until he could barely make out shapes and faces by his tenth birthday.

His disease had robbed him completely of his sight by the age of 13, the same year his mother had been traumatically killed in a car accident. For many children, these losses would have been crippling, but it left Erik only tougher and more resilient. His father continued to impress upon his three sons the importance of family, pulling the boys even closer to himself and each other. To the outside world, Erik's father and brothers were fiercely protective of their youngest member. But within, they didn't allow him to use his blindness as an excuse to stop achieving in his life.

He had not only achieved, but flourished. Academically, he excelled, earning a Master's degree in education from Boston University. He had landed a very prestigious teaching assignment at The Phoenix Country Day School. He had also continued the family's adventurous tradition, taking on long hikes in central Asia with the help of guides.

He was just beginning to learn about serious climbing, however. As a teenager, he had attended a camp for the blind where they had a twenty foot wall that could be scaled. He made his way up the side again and again, dozens of times in an afternoon, finding and testing different ways up its constructed face. Long after the other campers had moved on to other activities, he found himself experimenting with holds and movements. It wasn't much of a start, but it had given him an early love of climbing that he hadn't forgotten in the years since.

When he moved to Phoenix, he decided that he wanted to drive his love for climbing further. The problem was, nobody else wanted to go along for the ride. He joined rock climbing gyms and had good conversations with the other members. But once the talk turned to an actual climb outdoors, everyone he met was busy that day. He tried hanging out near the rock gardens that dot the countryside in Arizona, having close friends help him find his way up the sharp, red stones that grew there. Inevitably, others would be impressed with his skill. But again, when it came time to talk about meeting somewhere for a longer ascent, the whole world seemed to have a dentist appointment that day. Everyone admired him, but nobody wanted to be the one to get stuck dragging him around, or worse, explaining why they'd been with him if he got hurt.

In desperation, he started calling established guides. If he couldn't find partners the way other climbers did, then he would pay someone to teach him. Even this didn't work out. Once the guides got word of his condition, their calendars filled up. It seemed that he was never going to find anyone who would train with him until he met Sam, who was teaching at the same school. Sam's open mind and carefree attitude made him an ideal partner and friend. The two of them spent hours at the rock gym and outside on short pitches learning the fundamentals together. Now, though, he wanted to do something bigger and he needed a technically stronger partner.

I was starting to think that maybe he wasn't just a charity case. For a new climber, he was strong, and no one could question his heart. We did dozens of ascents that afternoon, each time trying a different feature that would challenge him in a new way. He sometimes paused, but never showed frustration or anger. He simply examined a problem and then dealt with it.

By the time dusk was nearing, I was so impressed with his attitude that I decided to take him up one last pitch. This would be the longest and hardest so far. It was a roughly shaped spire that crawled and cragged it's way up over 600 feet, at times forcing the climber to move hanging and inverted up a concave surface. Think of trying to climb up your living room wall and then across the ceiling. It could be a challenge for even an experienced rock rat, much less a rookie who'd been at it since morning.

I forged up the side, feeling the effects of the day's work myself. Erik followed steadily, never moving too quickly, nor falling behind. At times he would reach out, searching for the next hold. I started to provide small verbal directions. I never told him exactly where to move. Rather, I gave him general directions, allowing him to figure out the final solutions for himself. He never asked for more than was needed or became overwhelmed when the route was arduous. He just kept attacking, slowly and methodically. It was an impressive display, so much so that at times I forgot that he couldn't see where he was going.

At last we reached the top of the rock, and sat for a rest on a smooth, flat stone on the surface. The sun was retiring, and my muscles ached. I had been impressed enough by Erik's climbing to think I actually wanted to go out and try it with him again sometime. I gave him the good news, but his answer was short and impatient.

"That's great, but what are we going to do *now*?"

I was a bit confused. "Well, I suppose we should get down and have some dinner."

"Let's climb some more."

"Erik," I said, "it's been a long day. I'm tired. Plus, it's getting *dark*." I lifted my leg to pick some of the pebbles out of my shoes. "Look, let's get some sleep. I'll take you again in the morning."

"You can be tired tomorrow. Do you think I care if it's dark?"

I looked up at him. He wasn't kidding. He just stood there, waiting for me to come up with the next excuse so that he could convince me to keep going. At that moment I finally began to understand what climbing was to him. It wasn't just about doing something different. This wasn't going to be a hobby for him, he was out climbing because he *had* to, and this was a chance that he'd waited months for. Erik wasn't adventurous, he was a lunatic. He was just like me.

Creating a Vision

E ven after climbing with Erik that weekend, I wasn't convinced that taking him up a real mountain would be a good idea. More accurately, others convinced me. In my excitement, I told some of my friends and family about what we'd done, and about the chance that we could do something great together. They didn't share my enthusiasm. Instead, they were shocked to learn that I'd gone climbing with a blind man. "What the hell were you thinking?" one of my closest friends demanded.

He wasn't alone. While some were more diplomatic, everyone thought it was a bad idea. Didn't I know he could get hurt? What was I trying to prove? Why couldn't I find a sighted partner?

Doubt crept in, and I started to think they might be right. Still, I couldn't forget how Erik and I had bonded that weekend. I genuinely enjoyed climbing with him and truly felt he had the kind of strength and inner fire I could rely on in a tough situation. Without me, I wondered if he would ever get his chance to do some real mountaineering. I had seemed to be his best prospect so far, and it had taken him several months and a drive to California just to find someone who would even spend an afternoon rock climbing with him. He deserved a chance.

Before he left Joshua Tree we'd had a conversation about taking this further. Could I work with him, he wanted to know, or would I be too afraid? My answer was truthful, but noncommittal. I told him I thought he was an unusually strong climber, and that anyone would be lucky to go climbing with him. It was the climbing equivalent of taking a number at the end of the night and promising to call. We both knew I might not get in touch with him, that I might decide I was also too busy to climbing with a blind man.

Erik didn't wait for my call. He got in touch with me by calling the store where I worked. He said he was coming through California the next week and wanted to get together for a drink. I wasn't sure I wanted to, but I didn't have a lot of choice. One of the downsides to being homeless is that you can't really say you're too busy to see someone. There was no way he was going to believe that I had other plans, so we set a time to meet.

As Erik's visit sat on the back of my mind, I went about introducing myself into the civilized world. I was looking for employment that would take me through the rest of the year, and decided to visit a friend at Berkeley while I checked out some prospective jobs in the area. While I was in town, he asked me if I wanted to go with him and hear a public speaker. I didn't have any plans, so I decided to tag along. Neither of us was that interested in business, but we went, mostly because it was free and there were complimentary snacks.

The speaker was John Scully, former President of Pepsi, and then CEO of Apple. I had never heard someone talk about business in a way that didn't relate to numbers and dry statistics. In his speech came what I will always think of as my epiphany moment. In a section about planning, he said "The future belongs to those who see the possibilities before they become obvious." I had never heard something so simple and so profound. I grabbed a pen from another audience member who was busy scribbling notes. I was so afraid I would forget this seemingly powerful statement, I wrote it on my hand. Even now, I'm amazed at how that phrase seemed to fit in with where I was in my life and guide me in the right direction.

Later that week, I met Erik at a small dive bar in Joshua Tree. After a couple of beers and small talk about his students, he got down to business. He wanted to do a mountain. Not a hill, not a rock formation, not a daytrip up a small face. He wanted a real alpine experience. He'd come to find out if I would be in for such a trip.

I didn't have to think about it. I already knew what he'd come for. His unrelenting pursuit of this goal – the same stubborn determination that had caused him to come to California in the first place and to return uninvited – wouldn't have allowed for anything else. If I didn't agree, he might drive back dozens or even hundreds of times until I did.

I told Erik to count me in, but I didn't just want to do a climb. I wanted to do something big. He leaned in. If we were going to do this, I told him, I wanted it to be about more than just getting up some rock. I wanted us to do something extraordinary together.

"Let's not just create a goal," I blurted out. "Let's make a … vision." The word seemed to hang in the air. *Had I just told a blind man I wanted to create a vision?* The thought, coupled with the beers, made me start to giggle. I bit my lip and tried to stay silent. I wondered if he could hear me trying not to laugh. What would that sound like, and would he know the sound?

Erik leaned back and seemed to take this in. I couldn't tell if he was thinking about what I'd said, or was insulted by my insensitivity. After a moment he leaned forward. I waited anxiously for his words, but before he could speak he just broke into laughter. Leaning forward and grabbing his stomach through heavy chuckles, the only word I could make out was 'vision,' followed by more laughter.

When we finally stopped laughing, we started thinking about a specific goal that we would work toward. Even more than his climbing talent, I loved that Erik seemed to understand what I meant right away. The difference between a goal and a vision might seem slight, but it couldn't be more important.

Vision, the thing that you conceive or imagine, doesn't have anything to do with your eyes. It's bigger than that. It's your sense of the world and what could be possible, even if it doesn't seem so at first glance. It's about doing something that might seem too far of a stretch, and then finding ways to make it a reality. It's having the foresight to see an end result in spite of all the potential hazards and obstacles trying to obscure your view, and then choosing a path to get you to the result.

The most important things I've learned about creating a vision over the years are to think bigger than you should, and not to be overwhelmed. It's easy to shatter your faith in yourself or a project when it seems too large, too intimidating. If you can convince yourself that it just might be possible, then it will become possible. From there, you have to take it in bite-sized pieces. Looking at the whole thing is often times too much to stomach. Even thinking about the next few hours can be too much. Instead, you just concentrate on the next step in front of you.

Most of my success in life has come because I've been able to hold a vision, by myself or as part of a team. I've always wanted to take on nontraditional projects, to accomplish things that there are no templates for. Too many of us lose that exploring spirit when we're young. We forget we don't have to do things the way those before us did. Pioneers can only succeed by taking on challenges that haven't been conquered or sometimes even recognized before. This means taking risks. There might be high consequences for failure, or maybe you don't even know what will happen if you fail. Hundreds of times, I've found myself pasted against the side of a rock, in a safe, comfortable spot. I can't see the next move, and my body wants to remain where it is, rather than risk the fall. But the only way to move forward is to let go and reach above into the darkness. It's scary and it's hard, but there is always another grip out there. You can either take a chance and look for it, or be stuck inside your own fear. There's simply no way around this if you want to do something extraordinary. You can't succeed, can't climb the mountains in your life, without the occasional fall.

Erik and I knew the risks we were taking by setting our sites on doing something spectacular, but we also knew we had a chance to change the way people saw us, and the way we saw ourselves. We decided we weren't going to just climb a mountain, we were going to climb the biggest mountain on our side of the world. We were going to Denali… The Great One.

To Fall is Human

With the goal of climbing Denali set firmly in our minds, Erik and I started to think of ways we could train for what would be a mammoth task. We had put this massive goal in our minds, and now it was time to break it into smaller parts. Although neither of us had been to Alaska, we knew we couldn't just show up and expect to climb the highest peak in North America. Some experienced groups never made it to the top, and plenty of them lost their lives even trying.

We set about training heavily in the Rockies. Nearly every weekend, Erik and Sam would drive to Colorado and work on mountaineering techniques with me. During the week, I would continue climbing and preparing myself mentally for the months to come, constantly guiding him in my imagination.

As fall turned to winter, the weather got harsh. We started to work on cold climate techniques, knowing that we'd have to face the same kind of ice and blizzard conditions in Alaska. As the months wore on, we decided that it was time to get out of Colorado and attempt something that wasn't in our backyard.

After scouting out some possibilities from maps and mountaineering books, we decided on Mount Ranier. It was

March of 1995, our first big climb together. Tucked away in the backcountry of Washington State, 54 miles southeast of Seattle, Mt. Ranier is the highest peak in the Cascade range, and the most heavily glaciered in the contiguous US. At 14,411 feet, it would be considerably lower than Denali, but the other features would make for a good introduction to alpine training. Also, the picturesque mountain made a nice change of pace with its aesthetic beauty. It has long, spindly glaciers that reach all the way to the base. Trees and sharp features dot the sides that lead up towards its peaks. The summit itself is the most magnificent sight of all, marked by two overlapping volcanic craters, with a crystal blue lake embedded in the lower depression.

Ranier is a popular climbing destination, attracting thousands of mountaineers each summer. Winter ascents, however, are more challenging and dangerous, attempted by only a few groups each year. We planned our ascent for mid-March, late in the winter season. The harsh wind and blowing snow would make it a bad place to be. But, we wanted to avoid crowded areas, and this was definitely one way to keep out of the way. When we got to the park, no other teams were around. We were the only ones brave enough, or stupid enough, to risk the mountain's blustery, winter temper.

The first day was all about suffering. The trail we followed would have been better suited for a Siberian Husky than a man. Only by slogging through mile after mile of thick, wet snow, icy temperatures, and frozen pine needles bristling into your face do you earn the right to attempt the more challenging sections. Step after step, my legs aching and burning, I crawled my way toward our first camp. I looked around to see Erik and Sam following suit. There was the distinct chance that we were going to freeze to death with smiles on our faces.

The second day brought more of the same. The sky spit on us relentlessly while we worked our way a bit higher. We were aware of little except the sensation of dragging our feet up a never-ending snow path. Eventually, we reached the second camp, a small clearing that would give us the chance to take up the technical sections in the middle of the night. We hurriedly set out our tents and small stoves which we used to make some dinner and tea, the only source of warmth we had. With the sky throwing wave after wave of icy flakes at us, we settled in for some hot tea and excited conversation. Once we'd warmed ourselves as much as possible, we buttoned down for a short rest. We had only a few hours to sleep in the darkness until we'd need to attempt the final leg.

Through the night, the strong, stormy winds nipped and bit at our tent, but we barely noticed. Exhaustion and excitement produced a light, but restful sleep. The small handheld alarm that we'd packed went off at two in the morning. We sprang into action, collecting our gear and readying ourselves. We knew that outside the tent it was dark and bitterly cold, but we were so anxious we could barely stand not to jump out of the tent without getting our gear on first.

Following a quick snack and a few moments to adjust our gear and headlamps, we set out into the darkness. Despite the fierce terrain, jagged rocks interspersed with brittle ice walls, we were making great progress. After the first pitch, we climbed through an upward field of massive, sharply edged rocks seemingly piled endlessly one on another. From there, we moved into mixed climbing, sections of scrambling over SUV-sized stones interrupted by brief pitches that required rope climbing, and a few breaks of just heavy trudging through the snow. A few hours in, morning broke and bathed the mountain in light. The sight of the orange rays breaking through the remaining pines and rocks above us was breathtaking. Better than that, the sun seemed to be burning through the clouds that had hung over us since the drive from Seattle.

With the weather breaking, our rapid pace carried us to the summit of Ranier only a few short hours later. We were ecstatic. It was our first big success together. We had come to test our training and readiness as a group, and had passed with flying colors. We paused for some celebratory photos, and took a moment to congratulate each other and bask in the fruits of our hard work.

Having accomplished our goal, we became eager to get back down the mountain to civilization. After days spent eating cold pasta from a can and frozen energy bars, we were eager to enjoy a hot meal and a warm bed. We made our way quickly through the difficult sections, scaling and belaying our way through the same jagged rocks and crumbling ice walls that had tortured us on the way up.

We'd already made our way through the difficult section of the descent when I was yanked off of my feet. One moment, I was walking along down the lightly descending ridge that would eventually lead us out of the park. In the next instant, my knees had been pulled up over my shoulders and I was sliding down fast. The area we had been moving through wasn't difficult, but the ridge twenty yards to our right extended down nearly five stories. It occurred to me that even if I survived the fall, that step might have been the last that my legs would ever make.

I could tell from the tension on our rope that Erik and Sam were falling as well. Sliding faster down the face and toward the drop, I couldn't see anything but white. The sensation of gliding over the slick snow face took me back to our training in Colorado.

On one particularly grueling weekend near Long's Peak in the Rockies, we'd spent several days preparing for this exact moment. I knew Denali would be filled with the hidden holes and depressions that could lie waiting just below the smooth ice surfaces. A single unlucky step on one of these natural traps could mean serious injury or worse. Sam had come with Erik out to the mountains in the dead of winter, where, day after day, we'd trek across snowy alpine valleys, tied together by rope. Unexpectedly, I'd throw myself to the ground and begin to glide across the ice, picking up speed. Erik, who would usually be looking for his next step, would be ripped from the ground he was standing on and follow me down the ice, our weight pulling Sam along for the ride. Once we had broken into a freefall down the glacier, our immediate task was to stop the slide as quickly as possible. For small slips, we might be able to use our crampons, or stop each other quickly using the ropes. For deeper falls, we'd attempt to drive our ice axes into the ground, hopefully self-arresting and stopping our momentum. We learned the real meaning of teamwork over those days. Slamming ourselves into the ice again and again until our entire bodies melted into a purple bruise, we learned to rely on each other, not just to stop sliding on the ice and end the pain, but ultimately to survive on the side of a mountain.

Now we were testing the trust we had built in the real world. The glacial ice flew under my back and then my side. I finally managed to roll over on my belly. My chin was facing down to the cold surface now, but I could finally reach my gear. With every ounce of strength in my body, I flung my axe into the ground and hoped for the best.

On the mountain, your axe is like an emergency parachute. You don't want to use it, but when you do, you really need it to work. We were slowing, but not fast enough. Desperately, I flung my axe again. Sam and Erik did the same. With a collective sigh of relief, we finally stopped.

I found my breath, and the strength to pull my hips from the ground. We took a moment to assess the situation and take a quick inventory. We were lucky. We'd only fallen about fifteen yards and no one was hurt. Our gear was strewn about the glacier, but everything was accounted for and nothing had broken. The incident had been just dire enough to freak us out.

From my new vantage point, it was clear what had happened. I had tripped, caught one of my crampons on the ice and sent us on the fall that nearly dropped us off the side of a cliff. What was my fault became our problem very quickly.

As I turned to apologize to my teammates, I realized an interesting thing. They were readjusting their equipment and collecting our gear. No one brought up why it had happened, or who should have done what. In the mountains, there's no time or room for blame. Time spent pointing fingers is time wasted. We had fallen as a team, now we would move on as a team.

I learned two important lessons on Ranier. First, there are no small steps, no places to relax on the side of a mountain. A single wrong move, even a tiny lapse in attention, can cost lives. Secondly, and more importantly, there's no substitute for a great team. Teamwork is the catalyst that transforms us into more than we are. Without it, we are confined to what we can get done with our own ideas and natural gifts. But by adding our talents to others, our boundaries are expanded and eventually removed. People can accomplish wonderful things by working together, but there's no room for blame or separate agendas. When you're roped together on a mountain, your fate is connected to every other person on your team. It was up to each of us to do our best, not only for ourselves, but for each other. By sharing the same goal and by covering for each other, we were able to reach the top and come back down alive.

Denali:
The Great One

That first trip to Alaska, in my mind, still feels like a vivid dream. It was so wonderful, so perfect, it hardly seems real. Like any mountain enthusiast, I had always dreamed of seeing the 49th state, but had experienced it only from books and stories. The cost and scope of such a trip seemed beyond reach. Erik and Sam had been intrigued by the idea of its vast beauty as well, and we were determined to find a way. After going through some of our options – the world's first bank heist led by a blind man, black market organ sales, a high-stakes roulette game – we decided we would look for sponsors. We had no idea how to approach anyone, but figured someone might be amused enough by what we were up to and throw some money our way.

Erik's dad, one of the most tenacious people I've ever met, took up the task for us. Besides his military experience, he had worked on Wall Street and knew how to make the kinds of inquiries and connections that could lead to actual funding. After a few weeks of scouting, he informed us that the American Foundation for the Blind, as well as some other organizations, would underwrite our expedition to Denali. Now, all there was left to do was climb the thing.

We flew from Denver to Anchorage in early June, still fresh off our ascent of Rainier, after doing some last minute training in the Rockies. Once we arrived there, I was blown away by the scale and beauty of the place. There were mountains that grew higher than any I'd ever seen, surrounded by forest that went deeper than your imagination.

From the urban comforts of Anchorage, a modern city poised on the edge of the wilderness, we set out on the road north, just over a hundred miles to Talkeetna. The small mountain town serves as a sort of pre-base camp for anyone who wants to go up 'The Great One,' as it was known to the native Athabascans. The weather around Denali is notoriously fickle, even in the summer, meaning flights to base camp can be held up indefinitely. Our giddy excitement melted into boredom as we spent day after day hanging around town, waiting for the clouds and winds to take a rest.

On our fourth afternoon, we found ourselves sitting again in the small bar that serves the summer's transient climbing population. Morning had brought thick, heavy clouds that draped the sky in a gray blanket as far as you could see in any direction. The small pub was crowded with a combination of climbing dirt bags and rich peak baggers from around the world, all burning the days and hours until we could get a chance to move. We were passing the time debating the merits of the moose burger versus the local brew when someone shouted from the street. There was a hole in weather. As we dashed for the door, you could actually here all the planes fire up a mile away. It seemed like the entire village was making a mad dash for their flights.

Once we reached the airport, the scene only became more absurd. Dozens of pilots were screaming at their passengers, trying to will their clients to get in faster, stowing gear and calculating weight at a dizzying pace. The planes themselves looked like movie props. Pure workhorses, they had begun life as small passenger aircraft that never grew into their extra horsepower. Like taxi cabs with garbage truck engines, they gave a snarl that seemed to betray their small size. All had been glacier-modified; they had welded-on skis where the wheels would normally be. Seats were removed to make space for extra fuel and baggage, and any instruments deemed unnecessary luxuries for the bush had been removed for weight. Like zombies in some sort of undead aviation afterlife, they had lived out their glory days as shiny, state-of-the-art aircraft. Now, they had been stripped down and armored in the hope they could complete and survive this one task.

Quickly, we crammed ourselves, and our heavy packs into the back of the plane. With the oversized engine already snarling, our pilot glanced our way and asked about our weight, and the weight in our baggage. Unable to hear our answers over the roar around us, and agitated from having been woken from his nap a moment ago by the other pilots, he simply shrugged and began to inch the aircraft toward the runway. I was guessing there wouldn't be any in-flight meal service.

The winding flight through the bush gave way to magnificent peaks. Exotic, surreal features surrounded us in every direction. After another ten minutes, the narrow pass known as 'One Shot,' appeared from the mist. Taking its name from the margin of error that doesn't exist, this small corridor between the surrounding faces allowed only a slight clearance even for the small aircraft that flew the base camp route. The pilots were known to say a small prayer before attempting to wriggle through, as several had lost their lives over the years. Once we'd cleared the other side, the glacier landing strip came into view. Looking more like a glacial tongue than a place to land a plane, the actual runway was a snow-packed trail sloping upward and ending abruptly with a stone wall. The pilot brought the plane to a low, slow crawl and touched down on the crunchy surface. After a few hasty minutes spent helping us unload our gear and supplies, he turned the plane and took off of the mountainside, eager to return home before being imprisoned by the clouds.

Just a hundred yards from the airstrip sat Denali base camp. The area was like a small city, with inhabitants from all around the world sharing the same goal. Alpinists from all corners of the globe were drawn to the mountain because of its prestige as the highest peak in North America. Throughout the sprawling collection of tents one could find climbers from the lower forty eight states, Asia, Europe, and a few from even farther away. The rich brew of languages and anticipation filled the air in every direction.

While it brings international flavor to the base camp, the attention Denali receives is a mixed bag. The fame of being the highest point on the continent pulls in many types of climbers, some who are only marginally prepared for the challenge. While lots of the groups succeed, there is a tendency to underestimate the mountain. At just over twenty-thousand feet, it seems less daunting or dangerous as several other prominent peaks. However, its proximity to the North Pole gives it some unique characteristics. Air pressure, decreased by the distance from the equator, makes oxygen much harder to come by. In addition, its artic positioning makes it much more prone to storms than other mountains at similar elevations. Finally, because it's located inside the United States National Parks System, a network of rangers keeps an eye on things. While a wonderful resource for those who need it, a downside is that people assume they will be helped if they get into trouble. In my later years on the mountain, I came to see firsthand just how dangerous this assumption could be.

Once at base camp, we met our fourth teammate, Chris, who would become one of my greatest friends in life. He was working as a guide with a mountaineering company based in Alaska. He'd been up the mountain a few times before, and was excited about the idea of working with us and helping Erik reach the summit. The idea was simple: I would guide Erik; he would be in charge of managing us up Denali. We had corresponded frequently by phone in the weeks before the trip, but had never met. As our plane turned and moved toward its departure, he walked over from his tent to introduce himself. With our sunglasses on, it would be impossible for him to know which of us was Erik. I was the closest to him, and decided to have some fun. Chris walked over and extended his hand in my direction. I did my best blind impression, pretending to feel my way out in front of me, and proceeded to reach out and grab him by the privates. As I shook 'hands' with him, the shock on his face was priceless. He had absolutely no idea how to react, looking from one of us to the next with a confused expression. After a moment, I pulled my sunglasses down and winked.

Chris fit perfectly into our team. Besides being blessed with a wonderful sense of humor, he has a natural strength and intuitive sense of how to navigate alpine environments. After the real introductions and some preliminary talk about our route, we set about organizing ourselves for the three weeks to come.

The climb itself was magnificent. The first day or two consisted of hiking up the winding glacier that makes up Denali's lower terrain. Because we'd spent so much of the past year either alone or in our familiar locales, I had forgotten how people would react to Erik. All around base camp and the surrounding areas, where we spent our days knotted tightly next to other groups, we would receive strange looks. Either directly, or out of the corners of their eyes, the other teams would spy us leading our blind friend along the path. While their skeptical looks were understandable, I worried they would distract us from the goal of getting up and down safely. Thankfully, as we moved higher the congestion of the lower altitudes gave way to more space where we could concentrate on the tasks at hand.

Oddly enough, our early trouble on the mountain was heat. Even though Denali is nestled in a range just south of the Artic Circle, the sun glared down on us at every step and from every angle, reflecting off the glacier that overwhelmed the landscape. The sight of so much sun coming off water, snow and ice was visually deafening. We were tiring quickly each day, often stripping down to the bare minimums of clothing, sometimes less, to endure the warmth. Ultimately, with the help of the Alaskan midnight sun, we started to climb at night. Dusk to dawn, we hiked and scrambled our way through a spectacular terrain bathed in orange, the sun lowering but never setting above us. Traveling at night proved to be safer as well. Glaciers, which move and crack under the afternoon heat, would rest while we tread over them.

Nearly three weeks passed as we moved up and across the mountain. We weren't the fastest team, but made better time than could have been expected. Erik handled the altitude and new terrain brilliantly. While the rest of the team soaked up the scenic views and passages that seemed to be around every turn, he absorbed the sights, sounds and smells you just couldn't find at sea level. For the first time in any of our lives, we had a sense of being on a big adventure. We were loving every second of it.

Our ascent was halted by weather at the final camp, seventeen-thousand feet above sea level. For three days, we waited. The summit was tantalizingly close, only an eight-hour climb above us. As we waited, we had to conserve food, aware that we only had a couple days' spare provisions. Worry began to set in, if the weather didn't break in a few days, we would be forced to turn around. Finally, on the third night, a massive earthquake (a fairly common occurrence on the mountain) shook the ground beneath us and freed avalanches that roared down the mountainside below us. Quakes triggering falling slopes of snow can be disastrous, but this one turned out to be a good omen. Deep into the night, the weather broke. We were clear to ascend the summit. As fate would have it, we left early in the morning on June 27, 1995 – Helen Keller's birthday.

Sam, Erik, Chris, and I set out eagerly, smiling beneath our down coats and heavy packs. That night was long, but we were all so excited it seemed effortless. I don't think any of us could believe we were really going to make it. As our triumph became more and more inevitable, the buzz in my bones became almost unbearable. To control my excitement, I focused on one step after another. I went step-by-step, almost mad with happiness. Then, as if I'd reached the end of my neighborhood block, I was standing on the summit, the highest point in North America, with a blind man at my side.

The local NBC affiliate had sent an airplane up to film us for coverage on NBC Nightly News. Standing on the peak, we could hear it flying in the distance, circling our position. As we waved hello to what we imagined would be our new, adoring fans, Erik leaned over and asked, "Do you think they'll know which one I am?" It would be hard to tell with all of us wearing the same red suits.

"Sure." I replied. "You're the only one waving in the wrong direction."

With a chuckle, I turned my friend around toward the plane and we shared a spectacular moment, the culmination of all our hard work. It would be the first of many to come in the following years.

Positive Pessimism

Mountain climbing is a perverse endeavor. It takes a different kind of person to decide they would rather drag themselves through days or weeks of pain on the side of some cold rock than stay at home in a warm bed with their loved ones. Depending on your point of view, we either have a unique idea of a good time or a massive personality defect. Either way, a side effect of the lifestyle is the development of a sick sense of humor. Part of it has to do with the climbing machismo, but part of it is a normal human response to the pain and misery we put ourselves through. Positive pessimism is a great example. It's an idea we came up with accidentally, but it has served us well over the years.

The idea began on our trip to Denali. Being stuck at high camp was a miserable time. We were parked on the only spot with any real cover, a relatively flat patch of hard rock and ice beneath a stone outcropping. We sat around for days eating cold food out of tin cans, waiting for the weather to break. Sleep was nearly impossible, with the whipping winds and tough ground doing their best to keep us awake. When we were able to catch some rest, we'd often wake up to find that the ice beneath us had melted into a small glacial pool, or that the smell of unwashed bodies in the tent had become unbearable. We'd all had it.

By the third afternoon, I wondered if we would start to crack. In order to break the tedium, we decided to press on. We'd been hoping to make some headway despite the storm, but didn't seem to be making any progress upward. Chris was leading us up a dark, miserable glacier, when he turned and uttered, "It's cold out here, but at least it's windy." A slow smile curled up from the corner of his mouth. In spite of our shared tension, each of us chuckled for a moment.

"We've been climbing all day, but at least we're lost," Erik added. This brought a new round of laughs.

"Last night, I found a hole in my sleeping bag, but at least I got frostbite," was my contribution.

Sam had left us minutes before to relieve himself off the trail. But now, from twenty yards away, we could hear him shout, "It's twenty below, but at least I'm partially naked!"

For the next few days, whenever the team seemed to be down, someone would invent a new positive pessimism. For us, it became a way to laugh at ourselves and the downside of a unpleasant reality. Things aren't always great; they won't always be how you want them to be. The best thing to do is laugh.

I think learning not to take ourselves so seriously has been a secret of our success, and other people seem to agree. Ever since I first mentioned it in a speech years ago, the response has been overwhelming. Nearly every day I get a note from someone who is taking the idea of positive pessimism and making it work for them: *'I get micromanaged, but at least my boss is an idiot.'* Or *'The company is downsizing, but at least my assistant is still worthless.'* I think it's great. The next time you find yourself in a tough spot, try to find the fun in it.

And remember, life may be hard, but at least you'll die in the end.

Tackling the Tooth

ifteen miles southeast of Denali is another famous mountaineering destination. Like the Diamond in Colorado, the Moose's Tooth is not familiar to tourists, but many climbers are familiar with it. Also, like the Diamond, it has a name that seems wholly appropriate. A giant granite mountain jutting out from the Alaska Range, it looks like a broken tooth protruding from the glaciated terrain around it. A stone face flanked by white couloirs, deep gorges packed in with snow and ice, completes the image.

'The Tooth' sits like a little sister, scowling and defiant to all who climb her larger, more popular sibling. While not nearly as high, it has an intense and demanding geometry that make for a faster, but tougher climb. As the pilot had explained to me on our flight from Talkeetna to Denali base camp, it's a place "to test your manhood." I'd dismissed the shorter peak, staring me down from our aircraft window, as a curiosity. But now, a year later, I found myself aching to try it.

I rounded up a couple of my Colorado climbing buddies, Jon and Chad. After hearing all of my stories from Denali for a year, they were anxious to give Alaska a try themselves. We gathered up the money we'd need for airfare and supplies and started making preparations. Once May came around, we were on our way.

The journey through Anchorage and to the small village of Talkeenta was as breathtaking as I'd remembered. Just being back in Alaska was invigorating, and my travel partners were obviously soaking it up as well. I could see their eyes widen every time we passed into a new scenic area, as enraptured with the expansive backcountry as I was. Upon reaching our destination, we were blessed with clear weather. Not wanting to squander the opportunity, we departed as quickly as possible on our flight into the wilderness.

Our flight to Moose's Tooth was similar to the trip to Denali base camp. The same kind of glacier-modified plane rose gingerly into the air, pulling us through the sky over forests and lakes until we were in the midst of crystal peaks and snow-packed ridges. This time, however, instead of continuing toward the mountain dominating the horizon ahead, we turned north and touched down on a rugged strip of ice no more than a quarter-mile long. A far cry from the cosmopolitan feel of Denali base camp, we were utterly alone on the Ruth Glacier. I couldn't be sure, but I was pretty convinced we'd reached the actual geographic middle of nowhere. Once we'd unloaded our few small bags of gear and the plane made its hasty exit, there was absolutely no one but the three of us. We had four days to get up and down. After that, the pilot would come back and pick us up, if he could.

Between the glacier where we landed and the site of our first camp was a huge crevasse field. Beneath the seemingly flat, snow-packed surface were huge holes in the earth, hiding like landmines. We roped together tightly and navigated from one area to the next, our eyes and ears straining to detect any hint of a crack in the ice.

Three nerve-wracking hours later, we reached our campsite

and set up our tent. Sleep was hard to come by. Like skydivers who had just reached the ground, we were too wired to relax. The three of us, isolated and alone in the treacherous wilderness, spent most of the night in a giddy daze. We considered continuing our ascent through the night, but the sounds of avalanches tumbling above and around us dismissed the notion.

Finally, morning came and we were free to head up the mountain. We roped up and started into the long slopes of snow and toward the vertical pitches. With our crampons biting into the hard snow before us, we gently traversed our course, gradually working our way upward. The packed snow below us seemed to be in better shape than could be expected, but I was still wary. As the most experienced climber in the group, I felt I should point out and avoid potential hazards, even if it seemed trivial. After a couple of hours, Jon and Chad seemed to be tiring of my cautious mother routine, rolling their eyes slightly as I'd advise moving more slowly here or taking extra precaution there.

And so, as we approached a benign-looking patch of thickly packed, frozen-over snow, I asked Jon to plant a picket. The long spike, with a hole for our rope to pass through, would help to arrest us in the event of a fall. Jon shrugged impatiently and planted it into the ground. With our precaution in place, the team began to move forward. I led the way, followed by Jon, with Chad in the rear.

I was through the small patch and examining the route ahead when I heard the faint crack. Before I could turn and tell Jon to stay still, snow had rushed beneath my knees and was carrying me down the ridge. The rope tugged and released as our picket was ripped from the ground, unable to support the full weight of three climbers.

My mind raced to assess the danger of the fall we were in. The slope wasn't extreme; there was no risk of falling off of any cliff or ridge. Still, the sheer volume of powder falling into us and picking up speed had me concerned. It was lighter as it sped down the hill, but once we stopped, the molecules would condense. What was now light and fluffy would become heavy and thick, like concrete. If it covered our heads, we'd surely suffocate. Worse yet, if it buried us to our elbows we'd be unable to dig out – we'd freeze to death, and be awake the whole time. I wasn't sure if my companions were aware of this, but as I heard them struggle to stay above, I figured they had an idea of the danger.

I rolled over and attempted to swim through the tide, working furiously to keep my arms above. Unable to stay horizontal, I ended up nearly standing. Like a furious whitewater rapid, the rush of snow could knock me over, drowning me in it. Just as quickly as the realization came to me, however, the slide stopped. The tiny avalanche that had been triggered by the snow bridge's collapse was over. It had carried us forty or fifty yards, but we were none worse for the wear. I was only buried to my waist, and I could see that Jon and Chad were even better off than I was.

Using my hands as scoops, I cleared the snow from around me. I reached Jon, who was shaking the last bits of powder from his coat, first. We exchanged a pair of *did you see that* looks, and then had a laugh. We'd fallen prey to one of the mountains unforseen dangers and lived.

Chad, however, didn't seem to share our good spirits. The look on his face was one of shock. He'd come to Alaska for an adventure, but didn't want to pay with his life. Until that moment, he hadn't realized how high the stakes really were. I knew everyone handled these things mentally in their own way, so I gave him some space while I collected the loose bits of gear and food that had fallen off of me and were scattered around the drift. Jon did the same.

Finally, after a few moments, the three of us gathered. I pointed up to a spot on the ridge near where our slide had begun and explained that we could probably get back in an hour. Jon nodded, but Chad said nothing. I took my first steps back toward our route, reminding them that we'd been lucky and would have to continue to be careful. It was nearly a minute before Jon and I realized that Chad hadn't followed us. We made our way back over to him, fearing he might have an injury we hadn't discovered initially. When we reached him, we saw that his problem wasn't physical.

He looked at us both, one and then the other. "You guys still want to go up?"

Jon and I exchanged glances. Was he serious? We'd spent a huge amount of money on flights and preparations. We'd come thousands of miles to do this. The slide had been an unlucky break, but everyone was fine. If anything, the route was actually safer now that we'd already sprung the trap that had been waiting for us. Besides, the plane wasn't coming back for us for at least three more days. What else were we going to do?

"Well… sure." I said as delicately as I could. Then I laid out all the reasons to continue.

"I understand." Chad said. "But I don't have a good feeling about this. That picket shouldn't have pulled." He looked toward Jon now.

I could see Jon getting red in the face. He'd planted the picket, and he'd been the one to fall. Still, he could never have known that under his feet was a thin layer of snow covering an air bubble. I'd walked over the same spot only moments before. It was nobody's fault, and we all knew it.

I stepped in before angry words came out. "Pickets aren't supposed to hold three people. Sometimes they can help and sometimes they can't. There was nothing under that ice to bore into." This seemed to quell Jon's anger, but not Chad's fear. We persuaded him to go through to the next camp, which we could set up after a short hike.

Once we made camp, we sat down to talk about our progress and decide what to do. I was afraid that Chad, overcome by what had happened, would decide not to go further and miss out on his chance to take part in an adventure we'd been planning for months. But after more than an hour of discussion, it became apparent that he had no interest in continuing on. With no way to get back to civilization, he offered to stay in camp while Jon and I went on.

As reluctant as we were to leave him, it was too tempting an offer to resist. Chad would be safe in camp, and we didn't know when we'd ever get a chance to return. Two people would be able to move much more quickly than three, especially without the spare gear and provisions we could now leave at camp. After Chad's assurances that he'd be fine, we decided not to wait for dawn. We set out across the rock face into the channel of snow under the midnight sun.

Moving through pitch after pitch, surrounded by the idyllic oranges and blues of the glacial ice leading to the top, we climbed in harmony with the mountain and each other. The closer we got to the top, the steeper the face became. Finally, we came to the final challenge – a massive, sixty-degree couloir extending thousands of feet to the summit. The snow was packed enough to step and dig into, but not hard enough to hold ice screws, even at night. If we wanted to finish, we'd have to free climb. There would be no tools or safety gear to save us, we were at the mercy of our hands and our feet.

Without a word, I began to make the first step. After twelve hours of scratching and clawing our way upward, Jon and I had reached an understanding. We were going to the top. Nothing was going to stop us.

After a few moves up, Jon broke the silence. "Be careful," he said. I looked back down to him. *Of course, be careful. Why would he have said that?*

All at once, I got his meaning. We weren't using ice screws to catch us should we fall, but we were still roped in together. If I fell, there was as much chance that I'd take him down with me as there was that he'd be able to stop my fall. I nodded to him and continued up.

For hours, we went on. We took turns leading the sections, entrusting our lives to each other. Morning broke and we continued to strain up. I was aware of being both exhausted and exhilarated, but the only thought that filled me was reaching the top.

When we finally reached the summit, no words were spoken. Jon and I both knew what we had been through together, what we'd both risked to make it to that moment.

When we finally made our way back down to camp eighteen hours later, I expected Chad to be sour. I thought he would have regretted his decision not to go all the way. Instead, he congratulated us and asked about our ascent. He was impressed with the story, but didn't seem to be bothered by not having been a part of it.

For anything in life, there are different levels of commitment. It's up to each of us to decide what we're willing to put into something. For Jon and me, the goal was reaching the top, despite the risks. In Chad's case, he realized he enjoyed climbing as a hobby, but it wasn't worth the heavy risks to pursue it as far as we had. That's all right. It's better to discover your level of dedication to something and trust in that, than it is to blindly follow those around you. Whatever you do in life, find your commitment to it and follow that to the top... or not.

Mind Over Mountain

My time in Alaska had given me a love of the place, and I was dying to return. Luckily, I'd remained friends with one of the rangers we'd met during our ascent of Denali. The next year, he invited me back to work on the mountain with the National Parks Service. I spent two summers working around the park – repairing trails, digging latrines, and rescuing climbers in need – having a fantastic time and saving money for school.

The following year, during the summer of 1998, I went back to Denali to work as a guide. My years as a ranger had made me familiar with the mountain, and I wanted to stay outdoors as much as possible before I left for The Medical College of Pennsylvania. I'd decided to return to school to become a Physician Assistant. While I was excited about fulfilling my dream of working in medicine, I knew the long hours in classrooms would be a far cry from the alpine lifestyle I'd come to love.

Chris was still taking clients up Denali at that the time, and got me on as a guide with his company. During one grueling stretch, we were scheduled to lead two trips back to back. It would be exhausting work to climb the mountain, return to basecamp, and then scale it again. Especially when you considered that we didn't just have ourselves to take care of, but also our clients. The energy we'd spend on carrying extra gear on our backs, not to mention cooking, giving instruction and keeping everyone as safe as possible, would ensure that it wouldn't be an easy six weeks. Despite the challenge, we were eager to get back on the mountain and meet up with our clients.

We arrived at base camp a couple of days before our group to begin preparations for the long trip. As we spent the first day getting settled, word got around that a Park Service ranger had fallen from a high altitude. No one could find him, but a few climbers had definitely seen him slip over the edge of a ravine. The ledge where he'd been standing went down several thousand feet, and there wasn't a lot of hope that he'd survived. With my years on the mountain, I knew how easy it would be for someone to make a simple mistake that could cost them their life. I hoped that he'd be alright, or at least not in pain.

On our third day at basecamp, the first group of climbers had arrived on the glacier and were taking in the pristine beauty of the Alaska range. The sun burned brightly as morning turned into a clear, crisp May afternoon. Most of the expedition were foreigners, and they were clearly excited to be on the other side of the world tackling North America's highest peak. As we took an inventory of persons and equipment, they chattered and giggled and laughed amongst themselves. Once we were satisfied that everyone and everything was present, we took a brisk pace through the path of packed snow that would lead to the first night's camp. Now that we were underway, their excitement was palpable. Then, something happened that would ruin our good spirits.

Late in the afternoon I'd heard radio chatter that a group thought they'd spotted the fallen ranger, but couldn't reach him by foot. It was eventually decided that the park service would send out 'The Denali Lama,' the Park Service helicopter, with a specially attached 'grabber' to try to retrieve him. The grabber was a valuable tool, enabling pilots to pick up equipment, debris, and even people with the use of a hydraulic arm that would deploy below the helicopter. It looked a bit like the arcade game where people use a mechanical arm to win stuffed animals, although this claw was much larger and more menacing.

From the air, the crew was able to confirm that the ranger had indeed fallen over the side of the crevasse. He was killed instantly by the impact, but had been lying frozen and face down for days. Now, the helicopter would recover him and bring him back for burial.

Flying a helicopter through the Alaska range, even without the grabber attached, is a dangerous and demanding job. Narrow corridors, unpredictable winds, and poor visibility can lead to accidents in a heartbeat. The talented men and women who fly these missions manage some of the risk by going low and slow through familiar routes. As luck would have it, we'd stopped our group of clients in a small flat area that lay directly under the chopper's path that day.

Our party, exhilarated by the fantastic weather and scenery, had stopped to take a rest and some photos. When we heard the sound of the aircraft approaching, the clients began to point with big smiles. They wanted to see the chopper close up. It rounded a corner and slowly floated into view. However, their eyes were not drawn to the shiny aircraft, but to the dead ranger staring back at them from a hundred feet up. He glided through the air, arms and legs still frozen in his bloody down outfit. For climbers, the mountain rangers are like superheroes. They're the ones who tame the hills and keep everyone in line. But as tough as this ranger had been, the mountain had chewed him up and spit him back out.

One by one, the smiles turned into expressions of horror as

they took in the reality of what had happened. And then, just as quickly, they each began to internalize his fate. After all, if this professional ranger who worked and lived his days on this mountain had fallen to his death, how safe were they? The unspoken question weighed heavily on all of them.

There was nothing to say, except to explain that on the mountain things could happen and, because of this, we needed to be very careful. I told them I'd been around Denali for years, as had Chris, without incident. I could see, however, that my words wouldn't take away their concerns.

No one who comes to scale North America's highest peak is new to mountaineering. All of our clients had done some climbing, and many of them had managed peaks much more technically challenging and dangerous. We still had the same experienced group we'd had moments ago. We still had the same great equipment and the same perfect weather. The only thing that we'd lost was our group's confidence, but we wouldn't be able to go all the way without it.

In the weeks after that moment, the whole complexion of the party changed irreversibly. The laughs died down. Everyone got a little quieter. Smiles turned to pained expressions of fear. Nothing Chris or I said seemed to make a difference. The further we went along, the more down our clients seemed.

As we neared the high camp in preparation for a summit attempt, the weather grew severe, as it had my first time on Denali. We waited days through the bitter cold for the sky to open up and permit us to reach the top. The wind and snow beat down on our tents day and night. Finally, the group came to our tent and announced that they would like to head down. They no longer cared about making it to the summit, they just wanted to return home. They had come from around the world for this opportunity, but now all they wanted was to get off the mountain and catch a flight back to Talkeetna.

On the surface, there are many reasons why a team might not succeed. Illness, bad weather, a shortage of supplies, or even simple fatigue can sideline a climbing expedition. Certainly, after days of waiting for the snow and wind to clear up, we had those issues. Still, they aren't what kept us from the top. The truth is, we had picked up another team member that very first day. With every step of every section, the dead ranger was going with us. Mentally we pulled him along each day until the weight was too great for us to bear.

The next week, we led our second group up the mountain. They were the same kinds of climbers, facing the same kinds of weather and challenges. But, three weeks later we reached the top. I truly believe that the only thing separating those groups was that one had their confidence shattered by an outside event.

You can inherit someone else's fear, or their failure. Any time you try to do something exceptional in this world, you're bound to come across or be reminded of those who didn't make it. It's easy to accept their fate as your own, especially if they seem to be stronger or more talented than you are. But no matter what their reasons for not making it, they aren't your reasons. You have to learn to recognize the mistakes and misfortunes of others without making them your own, it's the only way any of us can keep making progress. Heroes fall sometimes. That doesn't mean you have to.

Do the Right Thing

Towards the tail end of a Denali summer, Chris and I found ourselves guiding a dozen clients up the mountain in search of the elusive summit. Our group had fought through two weeks of sloppy terrain and the late summer blizzards that typically pound the mountain. We had just set up camp at fourteen-thousand feet, where we and our clients would spend a couple of days for much-needed rest and acclimatization. After fourteen days of hard charging, going uphill eight or ten hours a day with seventy pounds strapped to my back, I was relieved to be resting. I could tell from the way Chris was moving as we settled our clients in and prepared our own tent that the long climbing season was catching up with him as well. Once we had melted some snow for fresh water and prepared dinner for everyone we finally crawled into our bags for some sleep.

After about an hour of the kind of clear, sound sleep that only utter exhaustion can produce, I woke up to hear a clamor around camp. I wondered which of our clients would be up and making so much noise in the night. As my attention slowly came back to the waking world, I could make out Roger Robinson's voice. Roger was head of all the rangers in Denali National Park, the man responsible for keeping the park and its staff functioning smoothly. I'd come to know him well over the years. If he was excited about something, it was important.

I crawled out of my bag hoping to help Roger find what he needed and fade back into slumber as quickly as possible. But before I could get my boots on and step outside, he was zipping open the entrance to our tent. He'd heard Chris and I were on the hill and had come to ask a favor.

"I'm sorry to bother you guys," he blurted out, "but we're short on people and we need some help."

I stirred Chris awake as he explained the situation. A pair of climbers had reported a fall down a route called the 'Orient Express.' Denali had several sections that were notorious for falls. The rangers had given each of them colorful names based on the origins of climbers who frequently fell down them. In addition to the Orient Express, the Autobahn and the Champs Elysées were frequent trouble spots.

This accident seemed to have happened like most on the mountain do. The team had reached the summit and failed to maintain their focus on the descent. As a result, one of the members had slipped and gone over a ledge into a half-mile freefall. The park rangers were shorthanded, and they needed help retrieving and treating the injured.

As tired as we were, we knew we had to go. Mountaineers work by a code that basically amounts to the Golden Rule: you help out those who need it, no matter what. It's a dangerous sport, and we try to look out for each other for two reasons. First, it's the right thing to do; but secondly, and just as important, is that you never know when you'll need help yourself. So without delay, Chris and I dressed as quickly as possible and gathered a minimal amount of gear to bring on the four-hour trek to the area where the climbers had landed. I felt anxious about explaining our departure to our clients. They had spent large amounts of money for us to be there, and now we needed to leave them for the night. To my great relief however, they immediately understood and said they would fend for themselves until morning.

It was approaching midnight as Chris and I climbed up the icy slopes several hundred vertical yards between our camp and the fall zone. The midnight sun hung low on the horizon, throwing a blue glow off the surface for miles in any direction. When we arrived at the depression where the fallen climber had settled, we saw that a 'hasty team', a group of mountain EMT's carrying light medical equipment, had just arrived. Both of the climbers were breathing, but one had massive internal injuries and would need to be evacuated right way. The other, despite having some assorted injuries, including a shattered ankle, at least seemed to be in stable condition.

As difficult as it is to make your way up or across a mountain like Denali, it's that much tougher to carry someone else along with you. The series of pitches that had taken us four hours to manage on the first leg had to be traversed at a painfully slow pace on our return. Some sections had to be avoided altogether, as we wouldn't be able to move through with an immobilized patient. Others simply required small steps and minute movements to find a way without jostling the injured man or harming ourselves in the process. Like snails moving through sand, we inched our way along until at last we were able to deposit the patient at the high camp medical tent. By the time we'd made the short walk back to our own tent, more than eighteen hours had past. Our clients had taken care of themselves well enough, but we had missed our rest day. There was nothing to do except catch a few hours of sleep before we broke camp in the morning. Once again our rest was short-lived.

Just as I was settling into my bag, before I even had time to close my eyes, I heard Roger's voice again. I ignored it for a moment, thinking I must have been hearing things out of exhaustion. But when I heard him call a second time, I realized he had returned to our camp. I stuck my head out of my tent to see him approaching.

"Guys, I am so sorry. Look, I know how wiped out you are, but there's been another fall. Sounds as if a few Brits have fallen down the same section of the 'Orient Express'."

Without a word, Chris and I made ready to leave once more. A few of our clients had overheard and offered that no explanation was needed. They would simply wait until we could return. As the sun made its way nearer to the horizon, we set out again through the blue fields and walls of ice in front of us toward the injured party.

Amazingly, the injured pair had landed in nearly the same spot as we'd been the night before. The two victims were members of the British Army who had come to the mountain as part of a military climbing exercise. In a perverse showing of the buddy system, one had fallen, taking his roped-in partner with him. Together, they'd slid down the steep face and were less than a hundred yards from our previous patients. I couldn't believe it. The odds of two pairs of climbers slipping at precisely the same point, falling thousands of feet while careening off of rocks, ice and other features, and then landing in the same depression had to be astronomical.

We caught up to the hasty team en route and could see the bodies lying motionless less than twenty-five feet from the first fall. Despite their good fortune of falling onto a bed of powder, neither seemed to be moving. Moreover, the streaks of blood marking their path downward weren't encouraging.

Cold and exhausted, the four of us stopped to take a better look. Through high-powered binoculars we could observe them. For the five minutes we peered through the lenses, neither so much as moved. I sighed. It was unfortunate that we wouldn't be able to save them, but accidents on the mountain weren't uncommon. During the busy summer months, there could be as many as three falls a week. If these guys hadn't made it, we'd send a helicopter when the weather was clear.

We were about to leave the hasty team to go forward and confirm the victims' fate when one of the medics yelled out. An unusual mix of shock and amusement came over his face. "You'll never believe this," he exclaimed as he handed me his binoculars.

If I hadn't seen it with my own eyes, I wouldn't have. The smaller climber had stood up and was shaking his head. He looked severely disoriented, but he was actually standing on his own two feet.

We yelled at the top of our lungs for him to stop, but he either couldn't hear us or didn't register our words. He began taking one shaky step after another, bumbling his way forward. What had begun as amazing was about to end tragically. He was in a daze, walking straight toward a ledge five yards in front of him. We kept screaming as he continued shuddering forward. Suddenly he stopped, as if realizing what he was about to do, and teetered backward. We all let out a sigh of relief. Then, without warning or hesitation, he took a step forward and disappeared into a crack below. We couldn't see where he'd fallen, but it didn't seem important. He'd been lucky once, but ultimately, not lucky enough.

Still, we wondered about his companion. After all, if the shorter climber had survived, perhaps his partner had as well. We gathered up our gear and began to climb our way toward his body. About two minutes later, with roughly half a mile separating us from the spot where they'd landed, Chris stopped mid-step and uttered a profanity.

I followed his gaze until I realized what he saw and threw out a four letter tribute of my own. The shorter climber was up again. He'd survived a nearly 3,000 foot fall, gotten up to walk, fallen off a 45 foot ice cliff, and now was making his way toward us. We screamed frantically at him to stay still, but our words didn't seem to find him. He simply stumbled forward with a blank expression on his face.

Now just a couple hundred yards in the distance, we allowed ourselves to consider the possibility that he might make it to us. We set about navigating our way through the fragile ice field with its cracks, holes and false surfaces, all the while shouting at the top of our lungs. With every ounce of volume and strength we could find, we begged him to stay put. We nearly reached him, no more than sixty feet away, when he vanished. It was as if a trap door had opened beneath his feet. He had stepped on a snow bridge and it gave way, trapping him in a cold pit that might extend down ten feet, or hundreds of yards.

We scrambled over to the depression and looked inside. I saw something that will stay with me until the day I die. The small man, battered and disoriented, was using his frozen hands like ice axes. He chipped away at the snow and ice around him, clawing his way up to the top of the ridge. He had lost all conscious thought and was driving forward on pure instinct. After some quick rope work, Chris and I were able to pull him up and sit him down on the ground. Then, as we had the night before, we bandaged and packaged the patient as best we could and made our way back to the medical tent at camp.

More by luck than skill, he survived the ordeal. We found out later that he had just been married in England, and the thought of losing his new wife was too much for him. Even now, I'm taken aback when I think of the grit and determination he showed. That man was going to walk back to base camp no matter how many cliffs were in his way. Just as shocking, his partner escaped the fall with nothing more than a shattered ankle and a blow to the head that had rendered him unconscious.

As gratifying as it was to have helped save a life, I was

worried for and about our clients. We'd been gone from camp nearly three days and were in no shape to continue climbing right away. The men and women in our group had paid a lot of money to try to reach the top of the mountain, and Chris and I had been keeping them from it. The small British climber had reminded me about the power of the human will, however my clients reminded me of the depth of human spirit.

As we dragged ourselves into the collection of tents where they'd been holed up for days, they greeted us enthusiastically. Rather than scold us, they insisted on making us dinner and tea. We were being paid to take care of them on the mountain, but now they had decided to take care of us.

For the next twenty four hours, our group waited patiently while Chris and I recouped from over forty-eight straight hours of hard climbing with no sleep. On the second day, with our bodies and minds restored, we led our clients up to high camp, and then the summit later that week.

I will always have a special place in my heart for that group of clients. For all of the money spent on the trip of a lifetime, they were happy to delay their adventure for other people they didn't even know. They understood what true adventure, and true humanity, were all about.

So many of us spend our lives in a self-absorbed bubble. We get too wrapped up in our own issues to even acknowledge the struggles around us, much less help. Mountaineers have always gone by a code: if you see someone in trouble, you help. It doesn't matter if you're one-hundred feet from the summit and you've spent seventy-thousand dollars to get there. It's the right thing to do.

It saddens me to know how many climbers seem to have forgotten this rule. The news has been rife in recent years with stories of incapacitated people passed over and left to die near the summits of Everest and the other big mountains so others, sometimes their own companions, can go on to make the summit. Instead of teams helping each other get to the top and back, there are loose confederations of people all pursuing their own goals. This is a losing approach to teamwork, and a terrible way to go about life.

There is a great feeling that comes along with reaching the summit, but a deeper joy that comes from being able to help someone else out. You don't have to climb a mountain to find a person in your life who could use a hand. The Golden Rule isn't just for mountain climbers, and you don't have to save someone's life to make a difference. Even a small sacrifice can have a huge effect on another person, and you might be surprised at the joy you find within a good deed done. When the chance comes, try to be a real hero. Stay focused on your goals, but don't let them come at the expense of those who need you.

El Cap: Lessons From the Big Stone

Erik and I took a brief break from hard core climbing following our summit of Denali. We needed some time to rest and build our strength back up. I had lost nearly twenty pounds during our time in Alaska and Erik had shed nearly as many himself. Besides, after a year of heavy training, we both had other responsibilities to attend to. I was off to school, and Erik had become something of a national hero. The piece on *NBC Nightly News* had triggered an avalanche of coverage from television, magazines, and the Internet. Everyone wanted to talk to us, from indie film directors, to *People Magazine*.

While we were grateful for the attention, by the next year we were eager to move on and try something different. Encouraged by our Denali success, Erik and I started searching for a new challenge. We decided to make a run at El Capitan, a granite monolith standing in California's Yosemite Valley. We had taken down North America's highest mountain, now we wanted to climb the tallest rock face. The timing seemed perfect. It was the summer of 1996, and I had just finished my first summer patrol in Alaska. Rather than go straight back to school, I used a bit of my savings to fly to San Francisco. Sam and Erik met me at the airport, and we set out for several weeks of hard training.

El Cap would be different from anything we'd scaled before. Unlike a lot of mountains, there simply aren't any easy ways up. Nor are there any sections where you can relax. It only rises about 3,500 feet off the ground, but you have to fight for every single inch. More than any other American climbing landmark, the stubborn stone face had a long history of denying those who attempted it. Indeed, for several decades after the first attempts at the summit, a climb to the summit was considered impossible.

It would be a change of pace from the last two years in almost every conceivable way. If Denali had been a marathon in the snow, then El Cap would be a sprint through an obstacle course. We had been used to training for a big, alpine peak washed in snow and ice. The only way to successfully summit was to bring big heavy packs and wear the mountain down until it let you crawl to the top. This would be a deeply technical climb in scorching temperatures – a rock maze of overhanging faces, fingertip holds and smooth walls that offered no grip. There were ghostly slabs that went up several stories without so much as a crack, much less a ledge where you could eat or sleep.

With an eye toward nearly non-stop training, the three of us rented a house in Western Yosemite. We devoted the next few weeks to honing our technical skills and adapting the methods that worked for us in Alaska to a different kind of task. Just as we'd known that Denali would test our endurance and ability to withstand the elements, El Cap would be a gauge of our raw aptitude and instinct.

We got off to a slow start. Our first target was a big stone block, protruding about 1,400 feet from the earth on the outskirts of the park. With its winding corridors rumbling right to left on the way to the top, it looked to be a nice orientation to a technical challenge.

We started up just after 7 a.m., alternating leads while lifting ourselves through the short pitches. The climbing was slow as each of us took our turns at the front, grinding up the sheer face that pinched our fingers and scraped our legs. By noon, we were just short of halfway up. It felt like the sun was beating down on us directly, as if it had chosen us alone to receive its torment. The heavy heat only served to slow our progress. I found myself tiring quickly and clawing at the rock with sweaty hands. The day wore on and we continued toward the top. A climb that should have taken us a few hours saw us reach the summit near sun down. We knew we had to descend, but fatigue took hold as we took in the last of our water at the top. Finally, the sun disappeared and we began to make our way back to ground. It was Sam's turn to lead, but in the darkness he couldn't find our rappel anchors, the metal hooks that we would slide our ropes through to lower down the rock. Sam and I searched for them with our headlamps while Erik took to ground, reaching out to find them with his hands. After a few minutes, the situation started to look bleak. It was the evening of our first day, and we were lost. As hot as the day had been, the evening alpine cold would be dangerous if we had to sleep out all night.

After some more searching, I nearly tripped over one of the anchors and we belayed our way down the side. Our spirits weren't great, but we'd been through enough together to know that every day wasn't perfect. So, without any words we headed for sleep.

We took an extra rest day after our previous debacle, and then decided to give it another try. We chose another rock that offered a similar challenge, and set out to climb. After a few minutes of preparations, we realized we were short some of the gear we'd need. Sam, Erik, and I debated for a few moments about who had been responsible for bringing it, until we finally agreed just to head back to the house and start over. Not wanting to lose a whole day, we sped back, gathered the missing gear, and returned as quickly as we could.

Only a couple of hours had passed, but by the time we started climbing, the heat in the park was overwhelming. The stone was scorching to the touch. Even worse, the pale granite was acting as a furnace, radiating light and heat back at us.

My thoughts became slow and sluggish. I found myself daydreaming about climbing the side of a baked potato. The thought made me laugh slowly out loud. Sam, confused by my outburst, peered up at me from below. There was something odd about his face, but I couldn't put my finger on it. He was bright red, but completely dry. I felt my shirt; I was dry too. We had all stopped sweating. We were suffering from heat exhaustion.

I quickly recalled my medical training and realized our peril. In this situation, heat exhaustion could be deadly. Facing the extreme temperatures and dehydration, any of us could have a heat stroke. We were miles from the nearest road, and at least an hour from a hospital. I hollered up to Erik, who was a short ladder-length above me, that we should take some water and turn around immediately. He turned his head toward me, but before he could reply he vomited. That was answer enough. As the contents of his stomach rained down, I started to wonder how long until we could get back home.

I ran my hands hastily over the vomit-soaked rocks, trying to find my way down as quickly as possible. Luckily, our slow progress meant that we had only a few short pitches to retreat through until we were back to our car. Once off the ropes, we huddled in the shade, making sure to empty our water bottles. We shuttled home for some rest, but no one spoke. Our first week had seen us climb twice, and both had nearly ended very badly.

Once again, we were forced to set aside a few days for unplanned recuperation. By the beginning of the second week we were feeling stronger and ready to hit the rocks again. We decided to make a long day of several shorter formations, going up and down while concentrating on basic technique. Our movements were clumsy, but without any serious mistakes. By the afternoon, we'd all lightened up a bit. With each successful route, some of the tension of our earlier failures melted away.

For the last climb of the day, we picked a tall stone structure with twists and curves that made it look as much like modern art as a natural feature. I led the first pitch, finding my movements more easily now. Erik followed, his strong climbing instincts returning as well. Finally, Sam joined us at the top.

Once we reached the summit, we paused for a quick high five and decided to call it a day. Mirroring our ascent, I was the first to go down, followed by Erik, and then Sam. Once I'd reached the bottom, I started to take off some of my gear and give a few verbal directions to Erik. Soon, he had reached safety as well and was belaying Sam down, who was removing our gear from the face as he rappelled to ground. With the day's mission firmly accomplished, I laid back into a small patch of grass, grateful for the rest.

While I was napping in the grass, Erik had been doling out small rations of rope to Sam, who would remove a piece of gear and then come down another ten feet and remove another. As the anchorman holding the line, Erik was the only thing keeping Sam from falling backward. As he rappelled down lower however, the small pile of excess rope was drying up. Unable to see the dwindling length on the ground, Erik fed Sam the last bit, which flew up toward the sky. Sensing a break in the rope's tension, Sam instinctively grabbed on the gear he was removing, a split second before it was too late. Had it not held, he would have fallen backward to his death.

My eyes opened wide when I heard the rope slip. I looked over to Erik, who was feeling for the safety line that had flung far above him, useless without the weight to anchor it. Sam looked an ashen white, hanging backward from 60 feet above. I was able to free climb quickly to his location with a new rope in hand, but it was too late – the damage to our psyche had been done. Our first two training mishaps had been dangerous, but this one came within an inch of killing one of us.

Shaken, we returned to our rented home. No one knew what to say or think. When morning came, instead of going climbing, the three of us headed to a local coffee shop. No one had fallen the day before, but they might as well have. Our confidence in ourselves and each other was shattered.

We had a long, heartfelt talk that lasted for hours. As my two teammates and I aired our thoughts and fears, we realized that we had some serious questions to address. Had we been lucky on Denali? Were we good enough to keep going? Did we trust each other enough? Were we doing enough to stay safe?

One by one we weighed in. At several times in the discussion, we almost agreed to call our trip to El Cap, and maybe any future trips, off for good. The worries and concerns that came up were all serious and legitimate. Sam wasn't sure he could still trust Erik to keep him safe. Erik wasn't sure he could still trust me to be his fail safe. I didn't know if Sam was strong enough to keep going.

In the end, we decided that we could beat El Cap, but we'd have to start taking it more seriously. This wouldn't be like anything we'd done before, and we couldn't assume just because things had worked out for us last time, that they would this time. We needed to keep a better eye on each other. There was no rest; there were no times to relax as long as any of us was in danger. Our team nearly fell that day. We narrowly escaped giving into fear and mistrust. When we walked into that coffee shop, I thought we might never climb together again. Instead, by being open to each other and recommitting to our goals, we came out stronger than we'd ever been.

Five weeks later, we went to climb El Capitan. The ascent itself was somewhat unremarkable, because we'd done the hard work needed to reach the top before we showed up. It took some trial and error, but we found out we could do something that, in the beginning, had seemed beyond us.

El Cap isn't one of the world's highest summits. It's not that high off the ground, compared to a mountain like Rainer or Denali. Outside of the climbing community, the public and the press aren't familiar with it. So when we reached the summit this time, there were no cameras or microphones. But we knew what we'd put in to reach that point. We'd done it just for ourselves and, as we celebrated our small, private victory, I'd never been so proud of myself and my teammates. The big victories aren't always the ones that people think they should be. But deep inside, you know when you've done something significant – when you've pushed yourself beyond your comfort and into a new area. Seek out those challenges, and don't be afraid of setbacks along the way. Sometimes you have to lose before you can win. A step back can be a step forward, but only if you keep at it.

The Royal Treatment

Not long after we'd climbed Denali, Erik called me with a strange request. Sarah Ferguson, the Duchess of York, wanted to go rock climbing with us. I didn't immediately understand. With the media attention that had followed our summit in Alaska, we'd made many new acquaintances, but why would British royalty want to hang out with a blind climber and his dirt bag buddy?

As it happened, Fergie had just divorced her husband, Prince Andrew. Seeking to reinvent her life, she was trying out a number of new projects, both publicly and privately. Looking to capitalize on her fame, a group of television producers convinced her to do a four-part series that would follow her around while she embarked on new adventures – a kind of royal reality television special.

Earlier segments had featured the Duchess horseback riding in Argentina and shark diving off the coast of New Zealand. Now, she was interested in climbing with Erik and I. We both agreed right away. After all, it was close to home, neither of us had anything else to do, and how often can you say you've rubbed elbows with the royal family?

We met her at Garden of the Gods National Park, a collection of magnificent, red stone formations near Pike's Peak in South-Central Colorado. After some introductions, I set about scouting the different rock faces we could attempt. I wanted to find a section that she, as a beginning climber, would be able to complete in relatively short period of time. For each possibility I pointed out, the producers would examine the route to ensure that it lent itself to the necessary aesthetic beauty and camera angles to get a good shot.

After about fifteen minutes, we decided on a short stone wall that seemed to meet everyone's needs. It was a ten story red slab with a curve up the middle that looked like the outward facing spine of an open book. The route was fairly steep, but there was a natural ledge about halfway up that could be used for a rest. Everyone was in place when our guest star got a look at the chosen pitch. She sized it up and down and wasn't impressed, wondering aloud if it wasn't a bit too basic. I assured her that, while it wouldn't be overwhelming, she'd be challenged to get to the top. A short deliberation followed, and she agreed to try it out.

I led the first pitch, crawling up the stone holds in a matter of minutes. Erik followed suit, moving casually through a section that was well below our skill level. Fergie watched us cruise up the side and seemed to assume she'd be able to follow at a similar pace. After a few steps up, however, she started to have some difficulty. About ten feet off the ground, the holds were farther apart and less obvious. The stones she slapped her hands at were smooth and slippery. It seemed to hit her that this might be tougher than she'd imagined. Frustrated, she reached out to find a grip and fell backward, swinging onto the safety rope. Looking annoyed, she pulled herself back for another attempt. Again she fell.

I looked down and tried to assess the situation. She was clearly struggling, but didn't want to show or admit her difficulty with the cameras rolling. After a few more falls, she managed to climb up and join us on the ledge. Erik, doing his best to keep the show going, asked how she was enjoying her climb. She replied that it was challenging, but good. Beneath her reply both Erik and I could sense she was in trouble, but not wanting to embarrass her, we decided to keep heading for the top. There were only about fifty feet to go until the summit, and Erik gave her some impromptu advice on finding holds and moving upward. It was decided he should lead the next pitch.

Erik took the short section slowly, not wanting to accentuate the differences between his pace and hers. Fergie followed, moving in slow, measured steps. I went last, watching her progress from below. Thing seemed to be going more smoothly until she had gone about twenty feet, at which point she reached out her arms and completely froze.

Unable to locate the next step, she had looked down towards the ground and become paralyzed. Sixty feet off the ground is nothing for a rock climber, but for someone trying to find their way for the first time with nothing more than a rope to hold them it can be terrifying. She was stuck, mentally and physically, and I knew I needed to move her myself.

I worked my way up slowly, not wanting to put her or the television crew into a panic. By the time I reached her, she was crying and visibly upset. Her sobs were interrupted by short, frantic breaths. Her bodyguards, the British version of Secret Service, immediately hit the roof. They were six stories below shouting things like 'abort!' and 'get her down now!' The added noise and excitement was the last thing we needed. She had a small radio clipped to her belt. I picked it up and asked them to be quiet for a moment so the Duchess and I could have a talk. In the back of my mind, I hoped they wouldn't decide to deposit me in the Thames.

Fergie continued to cry softly, while I searched for a way to help. I genuinely liked her and wanted her TV special to work out. Everyone was screaming for her to go back down, but that didn't seem like a great ending to her segment. With that in mind, I delivered what was probably my first motivational speech. "You *could* go down," I told her. "But I want you to think about where you are at this moment and where you want to end up. Think about how you want to look back at this day. Do you feel like you've done everything you can to succeed? If you head back now, will you be satisfied a week from now?"

She didn't answer me for few moments. And then, in true British spirit, she dried her eyes and looked up the pitch. I could still hear the bodyguards losing their minds below. She looked me in the eyes and calmly declared we should keep going up.

Once she had regained her focus, the climb came more easily. I reminded her to only pay attention to what was in front of her, not to look up or down. She made slow progress, often slipping or stepping on my hands, but together we reached the top.

Afterwards, Fergie told me that the experience had been one of the most powerful of her life. She got to learn about her inner resolve, and I made an interesting friend. She was so grateful for my help, that she offered to return the favor any time. I mentioned that I was applying to a Physicians Assistant program, and that a royal recommendation might help my case. A few days later, I got a glowing letter written on the Queen's stationary. I don't know if it made the difference in my admission to the program, but I never would have even gotten it if I hadn't just been open to doing something new.

Life can open strange doors for you when you just do your best at what you love. Follow your passion, and you might find yourself in some new circles. I never thought I'd get to meet royalty, but every year I still look forward to my Christmas card from Buckingham Palace.

The Long Way to Leadership

When I first started working in medicine, I had a mentor. Mark was, and still is, a terrific doctor who had consistently excelled at everything he'd ever done in life. He was the kid that most of our parents wanted us to grow up to be – an emergency room doctor with an undergraduate degree in engineering from MIT. Whenever I had a problem in the hospital, or in my life, he would be the person I would see. With his sharp mind and patient demeanor, there really wasn't anything he couldn't fix. A misplaced IV here, a weird test result there, he covered it all. As a beginning Physician Assistant, there was no one better to count on.

Mark had moved to Colorado in his early twenties to satisfy not only his professional aspirations, but also his taste for adventure, which included some casual mountaineering. His natural enthusiasm made him a solid weekend climber. So, from time to time, we would go out together for a long day on the rocks or to hike up a fourteener. He hadn't scaled the kinds of big mountains that I had, but he loved the outdoors and kept himself in superb shape. Despite being well into his forties, I found that he rarely had trouble keeping up with me.

Around this time, I got the idea to try a route on Long's Peak that had been near the top of my list for a while. This piece of mountain was one of the most sought after alpine routes in North America because it had a bit of everything: rock, ice, technical climbing and even some scrambling. I sent an e-mail out to several of my climbing buddies, hoping to get a party together to take a long day trip. I decided to include Mark, even though I felt it was probably a bit above his technical skill level. I was sure he'd be too busy anyway, and I wanted him to feel like he was part of my inner circle of friends, which he was. I also wanted him to think I considered him to be up to the grueling challenge, which I thought he probably wasn't.

Of course, I should have known to expect the unexpected. Not only was Mark willing to go, he was the only one. And he was fired up. When he stopped me in the hospital to remind me how excited he was, I was forced to confess that I thought the route might be a bit much for him. His only rope experience to date had been various short climbs with me in Boulder. He'd gotten to the top of several local mountains, but few offered even the slightest technical challenge. This attempt on Long's would be much more intense and trying. My reluctance seemed to leave him understandably confused. After all, I'd invited him. Now that he'd accepted, I was telling him that it probably wasn't a good idea. What kind of sense did that make?

After showing the kind of steely persistence that had carried him through a top medical school, otherwise known as incessant pestering, I decided to let him come along. I reasoned that his enthusiasm would be enough to carry him through the tougher pitches; that his attitude would more than make up for any weakness as a climber.

And so we met hours before daybreak to set up the side of the hill. At three in the morning a climber can easily feel one of two things – the exhilaration of starting off on a new adventure, or the sheer agitation of being awake when your body screams to be in bed. I wasn't feeling exhilarated. My edginess was coming through and Mark wasn't helping.

As we initially set out in the darkness, I realized his gear wasn't up to the task. Per my instructions, he had brought crampons for the climb. The small metal claws that attach to your boots would be necessary to make it across the first section, a ramp of packed snow that went 300 feet up and into the base of the climb. The only problem was, his crampons didn't fit his boots well. Unable to attach them to his feet with clips, he did what any engineer from MIT would do – he used duct tape. I was stunned. Duct tape might be useful for a lot of things, but holding the spikes that would stop you from falling wasn't one of them.

I wasn't sure what to do. Mark insisted his 'modified' crampons would hold, and I wasn't aware of an all-night mountaineering drive-through in the neighborhood. He reminded me that it was only 300 feet, and I relented.

I started up the first section with my tape-enhanced friend close behind. I got about half way up through the snow when I could no longer hear him following. Not wanting to lose my temper, I didn't even look back. I figured he would catch up at the base, and I would have a moment to catch hold of myself. Then I heard him.

"Jeff, I, um, have a problem."

I turned around just in time to see one of his crampons sliding down over the frozen snow, surrounded by shredded pieces of tape. Without it, he wouldn't be able to continue up the short patch without assistance. I continued on to the base to attach a rope that I throw down to him. Along the way, I wondered very loudly what kind of idiot would use tape on his boots.

After nearly an hour of strenuous pulling, Mark finally joined me at the flat, rocky area from where we took the first rope climbing sections. We were already behind where I thought we should have been time-wise, and I wanted to make up ground. The first two pitches were simple enough, so I moved through them at a brisk pace, with Mark straining to imitate my performance. I was in a good rhythm by the time we reached the third, and more challenging pitch. Conversely, Mark seemed to be reaching his limit with every reach and step.

Within a few more minutes, our situation became painfully clear. About half way through the third pitch, I noticed the rope going tight, and then finding slack again. Mark was falling from one of his holds again and again. Due to the twist in the route, I was unable to see him. However, it was easy to tell from the taught nature of the rope what was taking place 100 feet below. The rope, fully extended, would go tight for longer and longer periods. I said nothing as I waited for him to regain his footing and make some progress, but eventually the rope stopped giving slack. Mark was stuck, and I was furious. I heard several incomprehensible bellows coming from below, until finally he admitted, "I can't do the move."

It was a real predicament. We were deep enough on Long's that there wasn't really a viable option to go back down. The same crooked notches and turns that were hiding Mark from my view made a retreat more difficult, and more dangerous, than climbing up had been. It was much simpler to get over the top and down the other side. I yelled this down to him, laying out my case in short sentences, but he couldn't get past his immediate dilemma. I went through the reasoning again. "Jeff, I just can't," was his only reply.

My temper erupted. "*Can't* is not a choice here, Mark! You wanted to do this damn climb, and now we have to do it!" There was no answer.

After a few minutes, Mark struggled through. As he pulled himself to my perch, I could see he was utterly exhausted and defeated. The effort had left him so spent he had to stop frequently, even through the short scrambling sections. Each time, I berated him for his poor effort. The afternoon came and went, but we trudged through into the next night. Eventually we did make it to the summit, and arrived back at our car 26 hours after we'd left it. I was exhausted, physically and mentally. What should have been an eight hour climb had eaten more than an entire day.

As we settled into the seats, Mark tried to speak. He wanted to apologize for holding me back, but I wouldn't listen to his words. I cut him off, and then turned on the radio for the short drive home. As I dropped him at his house, I could see the wounded look on his face. But instead of staying to talk, I drove home for a nap.

After some sleep, I was able to get together with Mark over a beer and apologize. I had let my fatigue and impatience get the best of me. Being the great guy that he is, he forgave me right away and we've gone on as friends for years.

I'm ashamed to admit I let my mentor down that day. Mark looked to me to be his guide in that situation, just as I had looked to him to direct and support me so many times before. Being a leader isn't just about motivating people; it's also about knowing their abilities and limitations. I was in a unique position to judge whether he was ready to make that climb or not. When I decided he was, I should have made sure he was prepared and helped him through it. If he wasn't, I shouldn't have put him in a position to fail. Leadership is not based on a title or how many people answer to you. It's an attitude where you are constantly seeking out opportunities to lift your team up by showing them your commitment to them and your shared goal.

At times, we're all put in leadership roles. Other people in our lives count on us for guidance and patience. Learn from my mistake and don't let them down.

Spit Off the Top
Of South America

As we searched for a new adventure, Erik and I realized that if we wanted to do something bigger, we'd have to start looking outside North America. While our native continent is blessed with several majestic strings of mountains – Erik and I had done peaks in the Alaska Range, the Cascades, the Sierras, and the Rockies—we wanted to try something farther beyond our backyard.

Aconcagua, the highest point in the western hemisphere, was a natural choice. Not only was the Argentinean giant the most famous in South America, it would be similar to Denali in both duration and elevation. It would be less difficult to climb than its northern cousin, but shared the same odd pressure characteristics because of its southerly orientation.

Also, following our ascent of El Capitan, we wanted to get back to big mountains and ride our momentum a bit. The American Foundation for the Blind was prepared to sponsor us on another trip, and we wanted to take the opportunity get out of our sandbox and generate some positive publicity for them. It seemed like things were getting easier for us. Whereas before we'd had to fight through miles of skepticism before anyone would take us seriously, now we had people ready to send us around the world with fresh new gear and provisions. Who were we to blow a chance like that?

As the trip neared, Chris, Erik, and I got together to reacclimate ourselves with alpine conditions, drudging our way up mountains in Colorado and California week after week. Soon, we fell back into the rituals and routines that had served us so well in the past years. Over the long fall months, we threw ourselves into steep climbs and dreadful conditions, aware that we would see more of the same in South America.

The journey to Chile was long but engaging. For 17 hours I could barely sit or sleep as our flight drew nearer to Santiago. After we spent a couple of days getting acquainted with our South American colleagues, we departed on the eight-hour drive that would take us to the entrance of the mountain valley. From there, it was a three-day trek through the high alpine Andean landscape leading to base camp. In stark contrast to the base at Denali thriving with new arrivals, the first camp on Aconcagua was relatively empty. Although there were other groups on the mountain, most had taken the standard route. We were attempting a lesser-traveled option on the east side of the hill.

From base camp, I got my first glimpse of the mammoth we'd come all this way to stand upon. My immediate impression was that it wasn't pristine and beautiful, but that it held a striking, exotic quality. It rose like an upside-down 'V' above the surrounding landscape, exerting its heavy influence on the forests and hills below. I had a strange feeling staring up into the wall of glaciers we'd eventually have to pass through. Every climber will tell you that each mountain has its own personality, and to me, Aconcagua seemed like an old movie mob boss – docile and generous from a distance, but belligerent and angry behind closed doors.

My intuition wasn't far off. The first few days offered sunny skies and light winds as we breezed through the lower altitudes. As we made our way into the higher camps, however, the sun dried up and gave over to light snow. Increasingly dark clouds gave birth to thunder, then lightning. The heavens were in a nasty mood, and it was getting worse. With each day of driving wind and snow, our spirits darkened. The farther we crawled, the more ferocious the wind became, whipping us with small stones and throwing dust in our eyes. Like the Chilean girls I'd met in town, the mountain seemed to have a blustery Latin temper, uninterested in entertaining American climbers.

The second week became the third as we neared high camp, the final resting point before we could attempt the summit. We spent our days sucking down oatmeal, which we also came to know as *goat-meal, choke-meal* and *bloat-meal,* as we had on Denali, feeling certain the weather would break soon. In the nights, the wind reached speeds near 100 miles an hour, threatening to sweep us off the cliff.

We waited and waited. When our expedition had reached its seventeenth day, Chris informed me that he wanted to make a go at the summit. I agreed. As fearsome as the weather was, I couldn't bear the thought of coming all this way and not even trying to reach the summit. In the early hours, we set off into the cold. Even in the middle of the Chilean summer, the clouds threw down blankets of snow so thick we couldn't spread more than a few feet apart for fear we'd lose a member of the team. The morning wore on with no respite. Still, we kept hope alive as we made the way through our more sheltered pitches, hoping we could catch a break and steal a brief jaunt to the top.

A few hours after sunrise, we were at the point of no return. Ahead of us was a rocky bank that would lead to a couloir. The ice-packed channel extended up only a few hundred yards to the summit, but offered no protection from the elements. From our vantage point, it was clear the task would be insurmountable. It was unlikely any of us would survive the walk into what I could only describe as arctic tornado conditions, much less reach the summit.

We knew we had to go back, but still we deliberated. Shouting over one another through the deafening wind, we struggled to identify a way. It was obvious that a summit was out of the question, but we couldn't let go. Here we were, thousands of miles from home and 90 minutes from our goal. This was our only chance. Food and provisions, spent during the week of waiting for clearer skies, had been depleted. If we turned around now, our journey would end in failure.

In his wisdom, Chris said something at moment that I've always carried with me. Screaming to be heard, he looked at us one by one and shouted, "Reaching the summit is optional, but going home isn't." And with that, there was no more discussion, no more argument. We all knew he was right, and we could either live to face facts or die in a vain pursuit.

It had been a long time since we'd faced a defeat of this magnitude, and for a while I was angry. But as a few weeks passed, I came to realize that it just wasn't our time. Sometimes in life you set out to do something but you can't. It's hard when the reasons are out of your control, but it's just something to live with.

So much of our society expects success on every single level. We've made failure a taboo. It's easy to think we've lost because we weren't good enough or didn't try hard enough, but this is an illusion. In reality, a fall or setback is a needed event. Without it, we'd be complacent. What's important isn't avoiding failure, but using it as feedback. Cultivate an attitude in your mind, and an atmosphere in your team, that you're not afraid to come up short sometimes. Otherwise, the fear of failure will hold you back and keep you from venturing out and creating that vision. Fear will keep you on the couch.

After being beaten by the mountain on our first attempt, we regrouped a year later and went to the summit. It would have been easier if we'd made it up the first time, but we also wouldn't have learned anything. If you never fail, it means you're not testing yourself enough. It's better to put ourselves in situations where we may sometimes come up short and use those as a springboard for better things, than it is to stay in our comfort zone. You can make failure a habit or an excuse not to try, or you can make it work for you.

Finding Greenlandic Synergy

Gliding through the North Atlantic in a puny motor boat wasn't what I'd had in mind when we signed up to go to Greenland. Our captain would peek out at the choppy seas ahead to try and avoid the larger icebergs, and then whip his head back inside as the bitter cold bit into his face. Each time he ducked below, we could hear the hard whacks of ice chunks slamming against the hull. It would only take one good hit to sink us into the freezing water. I scanned the horizon for other boats, someone who might save us, but there were only rough waves and frozen blocks for miles.

We'd ended up in Greenland almost by accident. Just as Erik and I had begun to take our adventures outside of North America, we wanted to see if we could take them beyond climbing as well. We started to look for other ways to challenge ourselves while incorporating the skills we'd already learned. It had started out with a marathon in Cuba, followed by some longer rides on a tandem mountain bike. From that training, we began to embrace the idea of doing some adventure racing. The ultimate goal was to participate in PrimalQuest, a sort of ultra-challenge that would include climbing, biking, kayaking, and other trekking skills.

After some long months of training in the Colorado backcountry, 24-hour periods of climbing several mountains followed by 100-mile bike rides, we felt ready to take on an actual race.

However, before we could enter, we'd need help. Each PrimalQuest team needed to have four members. We'd have to find another pair who not only knew adventure, but were excited about the unique challenge of completing a race with Erik. We decided to partner with Rob and Cammy, two experienced racers who had approached us about entering a competition together.

After checking out some of the half -dozen races that would be held in the next few months, we decided we'd all like to see Greenland. Not only would the location be exotic, but the race would be longer and more demanding than many of the domestic competitions.

Our journey into the North Atlantic made me appreciate the genius of the Vikings. By giving Iceland and Greenland their respective names, they committed an advertising masterstroke and convinced many of their countrymen to bypass the smaller island and continue on. Our flight from Montreal had taken us into Reykjavik, Iceland's breathtakingly beautiful capital. The country was lush, filled with green life and hot springs. The capital held a cosmopolitan feel with its clean streets and shining buildings.

Our arrival into Greenland was a stark contrast. Our suicidal speedboat journey deposited us into a sparse and barren land. A cold, biting wind gnawed into me as we unloaded our bags. The only signs of civilization were the short, metal-sided walls of the small collection of structures at the end of a muddy road. Iceland's old-world charm had been replaced by the kind of décor that most would associate with a Siberian prison camp.

Bleak as it was, it would still be a paradise for someone who likes the outdoors. The country is rugged and pristine, largely unfettered with roads, buildings, or any modern encumbrances. Greenland is the scenic equivalent of the Nordic women you see in the movies —strikingly beautiful, but also harsh and very unforgiving.

Only eight teams entered the competition. Most of the others were professionals, competing for sponsorship and prize money. We simply wanted to finish the race and get our bearings for PrimalQuest.

The race began to wear us down immediately. The first day saw us summiting three different mountains. They were low, compared to the elevations we were used to in Colorado, rising only about 4,000 feet each. But they were hard-going, more like giant mounds of broken rock than actual peaks. For hours, we cut back and forth up loose surfaces, sinking and sliding with each step, to make our way to the top. After each grueling victory, we were left to hustle back down to sea level and take on another.

Worse than the terrain, I found almost immediately that I was becoming frustrated with Rob. As an experienced navigator, he poured over our maps to make sure we remained on course in the most direct routes. I was worried he wasn't taking Erik's needs into account. Several times we found ourselves mired in sections that were the shortest, by strict distance, but didn't make sense for the team. A straight line is not always the quickest route, especially with a blind team member. Without the benefits of my experience in guiding him, Rob kept sending us through areas that would be difficult for Erik, where we could have actually saved time by taking a longer route. I brought up my concerns, but he was convinced from his racing experience that we were moving efficiently.

The second day brought more climbing, followed by a long trek through several miles of rocky fields. After a couple hours of sleep, we broke camp and headed into a third day of hard mountain biking. The paths were sloppy and winding, punctuated with deep holes that threatened to drive us into the stones beneath us. For more than 15 hours, I steered frantically while shouting commands to Erik behind me. As I tore the handlebars right and left, he leaned his weight to one side or the other in tune with my directions. Every few minutes we'd go into a slide or a jarring bump I was sure was going to end with either a broken wrist or a concussion, but we made it through, barely, each time.

As the race progressed, I became more and more frustrated with Rob. Our tension was becoming palpable with each path he chose. He would calculate a path that seemed most direct from the map, whereas I would look ahead to the terrain and make a different assessment. We butted heads again and again, Rob wanting to take a direct route when I preferred another that seemed to take the same amount of time but spare us effort and frustration.

Finally, on the fifth morning we had a breakthrough. The team was roped together, climbing our way to the top of a glacier. We'd had a rough night, missing sleep to find our way through giant blocks of ice to catch up with the other teams. The sun edged its way over the peak we were moving toward, bathing the sea of ice around us in orange. The immense beauty of it seemed to affect us all, replacing our fatigue with a spirit of teamwork. At the top of the ridge, Rob called me over to look at the next section. A straight line would have led us through another field of crevasses that might have taken hours, but I noticed that by veering a few hundred yards we could save some time and effort. From there, Rob was able to plot a course leading us back by cutting through an outcropping that was barely visible to the eye, but clearly marked on the map. With that, things started clicking. We found that by looking at the tasks ahead together, we could get where we were going far more efficiently. We spent the rest of the morning moving through the barren countryside at a good clip. The whole team was in a great mood as we spotted the other teams' tents in the distance.

When we pulled into camp, we got some harsh news: we'd missed our cut-off time and been disqualified. Ultimately though, the loss didn't matter. Even though we failed to finish the race, we'd accomplished something bigger. We'd learned to work together. I had spent days thinking Rob was too busy with his head down, ignoring the reality in front of us. He was left wondering why I couldn't see what was being shown clearly on a map. It wasn't until we realized we were both looking at the same terrain but seeing it differently that we were able to function as a team.

As long as there are different people, there are going to be different ways of thinking and working. It's only natural; we're all good at different things. The trick is to pull together with those who are different than you and see if you can't complement each other's strengths. Sometimes the only thing you need to make it through the rough patches is a different perspective. Make a point of partnering up with someone who sees the world differently than you do, it might just take you off course and onto a better path.

PrimalQuest SufferFest

I will always think of PrimalQuest as my own personal nine-day tribute to suffering. The backcountry competition formerly known as the Eco-Challenge was infamous for the extreme strain it places on the human body and will, and we weren't disappointed. Erik, Rob, Cammy, and I were one of the hundred teams to enter the 460-mile race taking place around Lake Tahoe and the Sierra Nevada mountains. Although we'd been disqualified in Greenland, we were optimistic that we'd make a good showing.

The first morning started out well enough. We needed to navigate our way around Lake Tahoe in a pair of kayaks, successfully passing checkpoints laid out on the way. The setting was idyllic, with a serene dawn sky and water smooth as glass. We rowed at a good pace, each of us moving in synch with the other like a freshly tuned engine.

Our smooth launch was quickly interrupted. A few hours after daybreak, the wind picked up and the water beneath us unsettled itself. Our small boats drifted side-to-side as we tried to maintain a straight course. Our efforts were useless. The surface became more and more choppy until waves were rising above our heads and crashing down upon us. Erik and I paddled furiously just to keep the kayak from capsizing. It was hard to find any direction, much less speed. It was the first morning of a race that would take us over a week, and we were already fighting to survive; finding our way and finishing the race were secondary concerns by then. We simply worked our paddles into the angry water and hoped we were staying on course toward dry ground. Luckily, our path led us to shore in time to enter the next stage. Exhausted from six hours of trying not to drown, we crawled on to the next in a long string of horrors.

The remainder of the first day sent us on a run up Donner Pass, the site of the infamous early-American tragedy. Even in summer, the trail was cold and thick. As tiring as it was to climb uphill, I consoled myself with the fact that it was at least on dry ground. When we had finished the run, just after one a.m., we were rewarded with a mountain bike ride on the old Pony Express. The rocky trail had been somewhat preserved by off-road racers, but it wasn't in any shape for biking. Erik and I, trying to fight our way through the broken road on a tandem bike, weren't able to make the final stretch, a two-mile course that rose up sharply to a peak near the first camp. So, with Erik following behind me, I carried the nearly 50-pound bicycle on my shoulders. In that moment, it dawned on me quickly and clearly how stupid adventure racing was. It was to be the last lucid thought I'd have for nearly a week.

When we'd finally reached the peak, we could see other teams ahead of us. Relieved, we decided to follow them into the first checkpoint. After a half-mile jaunt through the rough terrain on the other side of the hill we pulled up to a camp… or so we thought. We'd expected a collection of tents and the trailer that our support team packed with food and supplies. As bad as the first day had been, at least some warm food and a few hours' rest were in order. Instead, what we found was a collection of a couple dozen racers scattered around the area, most of them lying on the open ground. I walked to the closest, a young woman sitting with her face in her hands. I could hear her weeping, and when I asked what was wrong she simply pointed ahead. I took a few more steps and then understood her pain. Where the camp should have been, there was only a tall barbed wire fence. They'd gotten lost, and we'd followed them.

Worse than being lost was realizing the only way out was back up the hill we'd just come down. Our team was too tired to even move, much less carry bikes up hill for an hour or more. We quickly huddled up and made the decision, as the other teams had, to simply spend the night at this spot and pick it up again in the morning. There was no room for sleeping bags while we were biking, so our only protection from the elements were the small foil blankets we'd brought for emergencies.

The four of us, tucked into the metallic sheets that looked like pop tart wrappers, arranged ourselves into a small dog pile. We were seven or eight thousand feet up, all of us in wet lycra, and the night air was biting. So, for the first (and hopefully last) time, I spooned a grown man. Between Erik and I, there is an ongoing debate on who spooned who. Aside from the uncomfortable questions about my sexuality, the warmth allowed us to get a solid 90 minutes of sleep before we'd have to get up and race again.

After the nap, we woke as the sun was cresting over the surrounding peaks. Ninety minutes wasn't much time to sleep, but it gave us a chance to gather our strength for the sunrise assault. As we rose into the frosty morning, the only way to keep warm was to charge up the hill we'd put off with the bike on my back. Two hours later we rolled into camp to prepare for the next stage.

The second and third days were all about biking. At first, we took the tandem through heavily-forested alpine trails. Those eventually turned into actual backcountry roads, which we followed for more than a hundred miles.

While the pavement was a welcome change, the lack of sleep was beginning to have profound effects on our minds and bodies. I was the first to begin hallucinating, seeing gnomes and elves that would scurry beside the road and hide behind trees. This was followed by images of snakes slithering across the trail. I knew they couldn't really be there, but still I was petrified they'd bite me if I stepped or rode on top of them. I wasn't alone in my delusions. Erik was conjuring up memories of his fifth grade class, urging him on and telling him he couldn't quit. I found out later that hallucinations are a common part of the struggle for adventure racers.

Seeing things was only the beginning. It quickly became clear why sleep deprivation is used as a form of torture. My head pounded and felt constantly light as we went on and on. We'd stocked ourselves with enough caffeine drinks to last a year, but they weren't helping. Each sip seemed more of an effort to get to our mouths than it rewarded in extra fuel. Erik and I had resorted to heavy tactics to keep each other awake. We'd run through all of the jokes we knew, talked about the race and mountains we'd been on, and finally, just punched each other to stay awake. After one such pounding in the back, Erik had been telling me some stories from his school. We were making good time, doing 40 miles per hour down a paved stretch. At one point, he got quiet and I wondered if he was choked up thinking about his students. I tried to reassure him. "It's okay man, let it go." Still there was no answer. "Erik?" He didn't reply.

Without further warning, the bike lurched to the left. It was almost as if 170 pounds of dead weight had tilted to one side. I started screaming at Erik as loudly as I could. After a few shouts the bike lurched again, this time to the right. "Did you just fall asleep at forty miles per hour?" I screamed at him. "I guess so," he replied.

His nap had nearly killed us, causing our flimsy tandem bike to jump left and then right at high speed, but I couldn't be upset. I was on the edge of collapse myself, terrified I'd nod off and send us into a neck-breaking accident. Luckily, rest wasn't far off. We got to camp twenty minutes later for an hour of deep sleep.

The fifth day brought an orienteering course. With nothing more than a map and our sleep-deprived brains, we had to navigate ourselves to a flag buried dozens of miles into some wild bush country. The hike was pure misery, punctuated by a run-in with a wasps' nest and an impromptu hug with a poison ivy bush. Our team was starting to look a bit ragged, and I was wondering if we would make it to our checkpoints in time. With only a few minutes to spare, we pulled into camp on the sixth morning for an hour's rest.

We were preparing for the next day's segment, whitewater rafting, when medical problems began to appear. For days we had been drinking lots of Gatorade rather than water. The sugar from the drink, sitting in our dry mouths, was beginning to form painful ulcers. Erik's feet were bleeding, Cammy was looking at a sprained ankle, and I had poison ivy in my Fruit of the Looms.

Still, we knew we only had to make it two more days, and we were determined to finish. After a short rest, we threw ourselves into the river for a whitewater rafting trial. Rob, who was a stronger paddler, got in a boat with Erik, while I got in with Cammy. Then, we set off for the five-hour trip down river.

It was during the whitewater section that fatigue nearly killed me. We had already made our way through the more difficult parts of the rush and I had become complacent. As Cammy and I worked our way through and around the rapids, our small kayak got stuck against two rocks. We were lodged sideway against the stones, with about three feet between them. Wanting to free the boat, I put one leg out on the upriver side taking a moment to note the shallow water, but moving quickly. The kayak was firmly pinned against the rocks. Without thinking, I put my other leg out on the same side and almost immediately after my foot touched the rushing water the force of the tide swept my legs right out from under me. I hung on from under the boat, my chest barely above water. Cammy threw her hand out to stop me from being dragged under, but wasn't able to support my weight against the tide.

I didn't know what was on the other side of the boat hidden beneath the water, but I wasn't eager to find out. There could be an opening, but there could just as easily have been another stone that I'd smash my head against. I struggled for several seconds, trying desperately to pull myself back up into the boat, but I was falling farther underneath, and I knew it.

Finally, my hands slipped off the side of the boat and I was dragged under. The second or two it took me to pass through the water seemed like an eternity. A million thoughts passed through my mind, and yet it was also completely still. When I came out through the other side there was no rock, only an open space in the water. I was able to crawl to my feet and dislodge the boat.

As anyone who has narrowly escaped death can tell you, the feeling is beyond description. In that moment, my fatigue melted away and I was overcome with joy. I felt such gratitude to be alive and able to have the experience of the race.

At last, we reached the last stage of the competition, another row through Lake Tahoe. Cold and numb, we climbed into the small watercraft and began to make our way through the water in the dark.

We were nearly finished, the feeling of relief beginning to wash over us, when we saw lights in the distance, both ahead and behind. The end of the course was a half-mile ahead, but a couple-hundred yards behind us were the boats of another team. We hadn't seen another party for several hours, believing the teams behind us had all been disqualified. But here was one more, and they were trying to catch us.

Rob, Cammy, Erik, and I looked at each other; no words were needed. After nine days of suffering, we were not going to finish last. We picked up our paddling, but the other boat still gained. They were clearly in a mad dash, as we were, not to be the final finishers. Our arms and shoulders were rubbery and enflamed, but still we tore into the water with every last ounce of strength we could find. When we reached the shore, the other team was no more than a hundred yards behind us.

We wept like children, overcome with fatigue and elation in our small win. After sixteen hours of sleep in nine days, I worried we might collapse on the spot, but we managed to hold on a few minutes to congratulate each other and the other final competitors.

I think PrimalQuest was a major point of growth for us, even though it might not seem that way to the outside world. After all, we didn't win a single thing. We'd finished nearly dead last and taken almost twice as long as the winning team. But we did press ourselves to the absolute edge of exhaustion, and still found the will to compete. We'd come to prove we could finish, and we did.

Climbing for Three

Like so many big things in my life, I didn't consciously decide to start a family. It just seemed to happen in a way that was so natural that I couldn't imagine anything else. I met my wife, Merry Beth during a Widespread Panic show in Colorado. It was a chance meeting, but I was captivated by her right away. Being with her was light and fun, but she also possessed a deep strength. The more we saw each other, the more convinced I became she was the one. So, after a few months of me being on my best behavior, she agreed to marry me. We'd barely gotten back from the honeymoon and were settling into our new home when my wife told me we were going to have a baby. I was overcome with joy, and a little bit of fear. I was going to be a father!

As any new parent can tell you, having a child changes everything. In the beginning, you notice the day-to-day changes. Instead of sleeping, you're awake. Instead of going out for dinner, you stay home. Where you used to worry about whether a dessert was bad for you, now you worry whether your house is baby-proof enough.

In the weeks after my son, Jace, was born, I don't think I slept more than three hours at a time. The whole situation was kind of ironic. I'd dozed during mountain blizzards, in airport terminals, hanging from rock faces, and even above the death zone, but I could barely get a wink with a newborn in the house.

Not that my waking hours were much better. My wife and I trudged through feeding, changing, and napping sessions together each day until we both started to feel a bit burnt out. Recognizing that we weren't going to be very useful to our son as zombies, Merry Beth and I started giving each other some short shifts away from the house. Those brief breaks did wonders for our mental health. She would use to the time to meet with friends or do some light exercise. I used my time to get away the only way I knew how – to go climbing.

My buddy Chris, sensing I could use a distraction, agreed to head out with me to the Flatirons. They were a familiar refuge that I'd been visiting for more than ten years. They weren't going to be a challenge, but they'd be a nice, quick break from mashed peas and dirty diapers. As we gathered our gear, I felt a sense of excitement. I hadn't been near a rock in months, and the morning was sunny and clear. It was the perfect setting for an easy climb.

With the ropes and equipment in place, Chris suggested I should lead the first pitch. Thoughts of my new son were still sitting in the back of my mind, but I was sure they'd melt away like my worries always did when I climbed. They didn't. I'd gotten about 50 yards up the angled face when I just stopped. My arms and legs froze, and I couldn't go any farther.

I sat for a moment, clinging to the rock, as a lightheaded sensation came over me. My pulse had quickened and my head felt numb. I reached forward half-heartedly, but my movements felt jumbled and uncoordinated. I wondered if I was having a heart attack or a stroke. No such luck. My problem wasn't physical; I was having a panic attack.

As I hung, it became clear that my problem was mental. I was bombarded with thoughts of my son. What was he doing? Was he safe? What was I doing? What would happen to my wife and son if I fell? The fears flooded my mind, forcing themselves forward one after another, until I was too scared to find my next grip. *I was climbing for three now.*

It would have been easier and safer to just keep going up, but my mind screamed for the safety of flat earth. After some deep breaths and reassurance from Chris, I worked my way back down to the ground. I was shaken, but not harmed, and after a few more weeks, I was able to start climbing again. I would never have thought I could have a panic attack. It didn't fit in with my image of who I was, having always been very centered and calm in the face of danger or threat. The idea bothered me for days; I didn't want to be a weakling or a coward. Then I found the truth – I was just a concerned father.

With that realization, I turned a page in my life journey. Having my own family to take care of made everything different. I'd sacrificed before, for my team or my friends, but this was on a whole different level. The game of life wasn't about me anymore. It's so easy to think of our families as responsibilities that slow us down or hold us back, but that's only half the story. While it's true that I'm more reluctant now to do some things that I would have jumped at years ago, it's a small price to pay for the joy that I get from my wife and child. Climbing your way to the top is always a great adventure, but remember that your deeper happiness is probably waiting for you back on the ground.

Thinking Big

The idea of climbing Mount Everest came to us slowly. In the years after we finally defeated Aconcagua, we kept looking around the globe for new challenges. We didn't have a checklist or a specific dream we were looking to fulfill, we just never felt like we were finished. Along the way, we'd picked up the idea of finishing the seven summits, the highest points on each of the continents. In addition to Denali and Aconcagua, we'd completed Kilimanjaro in Africa and Elbrus in Russia. There was one glaring exception, which happened to be the highest in the world.

Erik and I got together in May of 2000 to try and find the next adventure. We both agreed we'd accomplished some big things, but now we wanted to do something outrageous, something no one thought we could finish. This time, there was no doubt as to where we'd go. There was only one place, one peak, one summit that would satisfy us-- Everest.

Of course we were familiar with the mountain. As climbers we'd read all the books and seen all the movies. We had friends and acquaintances who'd tried the mountain and even a few that had made it to the top. But could we realistically give it a go?

We poured ourselves into the task of learning more about it. We talked about all the technical and logistical difficulties we'd face, along with problems we probably hadn't even thought of that were bound to pop up. In the end, we decided we wouldn't be able to forgive ourselves if we didn't at least give it a try.

To embark upon an Everest expedition is a massively expensive undertaking. Flights, gear, Sherpa assistance, and especially permits from the Nepali government are all heavy costs. Just to get there and back would cost more than most families spend on a home. We knew that in order to raise the kind of sponsorship money we'd need, we'd have to go public with our goal. We also knew the moment we did, there would be no shortage of people telling us it was a bad idea, and we weren't disappointed.

Within a matter of days, a small army of outspoken doubters came out of the woodwork. Many well-known Everest experts went on the record saying it was foolish and dangerous to try to take a blind man to the world's highest point. Many suggested, either subtly or directly, that Erik would almost certainly die, and possibly the rest of the team as well. They said we didn't realize what we were in for and, while we'd had some success, this would be impossible. They pointed out most sighted climbers couldn't make it to the top. They went on and on, publicly and privately. Erik and I must have heard a thousand reasons why it wouldn't work. We listened to their concerns, but we didn't agree. After all we'd been through together, there just wasn't room for their disbelief. They were experts on Everest, but they weren't experts on us.

Because we believed in ourselves, we found others who believed in us, too. It began with our families and friends, who pitched in from the start with emotional support and encouragement. From there, it spread to others who heard about our ambitions. One by one, climbers signed on to be a part of our team. Major sponsors, some of whom had never worked with us before, lined up behind us. Many had never funded a climbing expedition, but they pledged their money to help us do the impossible.

In the end, I think the support we got from everyone who helped us was worth much more than the money and gear they gave. We didn't want to rest on our past success. To go further and higher, we needed to surround ourselves with people who weren't afraid to do something that seemed impossible. They shared our vision to send a blind man to the top of the world. We'd set a huge goal for ourselves, and if we were going to fail, it was going to be on the way to the top of the world, not at home thinking about it

Sherpas:
Bad Gear,
Great Attitude

S herpas are a big part of climbing lore and legend. Ever since westerners began flowing into the Himalayas in the nineteenth century to seek adventure, they have relied upon the local guides to help them navigate the treacherous terrain. While a few Sherpas have gained fame from their own work, most often they are the unsung heroes of the climbing world. They're always present and they always do the hardest work, yet they receive little of the credit.

My first experience with Sherpas came in 2001 when Erik and I set off to Everest. I was immediately struck by how much they seemed in contrast to their western climbing counterparts. Whereas American and European climbers tended to be loud and boisterous, the Sherpas were quiet and reserved. We would share puffed-up stories of our adventures around the world while they said very little, except to occasionally praise us for a well-told story.

While I realized right away that Sherpas had a very different way of looking at things, I didn't fully understand how helpful and wonderful they really were until I had finished the trip and arrived back home. I had just returned from Nepal and felt like

I was still on the top of the world, literally and figuratively. I had gone to the world's biggest mountain, and with a blind man in tow! Wanting to stay in my rock star state of mind a while longer, I decided to take a look at some of the pictures our expedition photographer, Didrik Johnk, had sent over.

The photos told a great story. There were snapshots of the exotic places we'd seen, along with images from the climb itself. In one, we were crossing a deadly section of crevasses. In another, we clung to our ropes and axes while fighting our way up. And finally, there was a shot that captured us high on the mountain – striding through the Geneva Spur, deep on the mountain near Camp IV. I beamed with pride as I looked down at our photos, and was about to toss them aside when one caught my eye. Something seemed a bit out of place, but I couldn't put my finger on it. There we were, smiling wildly and being heroes. What could be wrong with that?

Then I noticed the detail that was getting to me. Standing in the background was one of our Sherpa colleagues. While we were whooping and celebrating under layers of high-tech, very expensive climbing gear, he was looking contentedly at the sky in a pair of blue jeans. And not even designer jeans, but a pair of knock-offs you'd find in a discount store. How could this be? I was bundled under several layers of Gore-Tex and goose down, all designed to keep me warm and alive in a place where life shouldn't be. This man looked like he was taking a stroll in the park. Mount Everest, especially near the top, is known as a 'death zone' for its extreme cold, wind, and lack of oxygen. True, our Sherpa friend was carrying a canister of oxygen, but it was for me!

At that moment, I started to realize who the real rock stars were. Our Sherpa friends had shown up every day and done everything asked of them and more, without the slightest hint of impatience or complaint. My recollection of this is not unique.

Every single climber I've talked to since, when asked, has vouched for the Sherpas' remarkable mindset. Their willingness to take on any challenge for the team without expecting recognition of any kind is an amazing trait. For them, nothing is ever too hard, too heavy, or too long.

Physiologically, many people think Sherpas hold a genetic advantage in the mountains. This idea was so compelling that a major study was done to examine them. A team of researchers ran many body composition comparisons between Sherpa and Western climbers, dissecting many of our basic human functions as they relate to high-altitude stress. After a solid year of computing and comparing, they found we are all basically the same. When I heard this, I couldn't help but laugh out loud. It just proved to me what I already knew: Sherpas have important qualities that are just not quantifiable. So how do they do it? It's simple, they outwork us.

They do indeed have something we don't, but it's not in their lungs or their blood cells, it's an attitude that pushes them to consistently overachieve. They treat every task as if it's the most important in the world, every person like they're a close friend, and every day like it could be their last. Sherpas don't do it for money and glory, they do it because it's a way of life. From the first to the last, they make it their mission to be worthy of being counted on. How much better would our world be if more people could adopt this attitude? In our world, it seems so important to take credit. Everybody wants to be in the spotlight, to get the biggest and the best. The real heroes aren't usually the ones getting the awards, they're the people getting it done every day. Forget trying to imitate actors and sports stars. If you want to stand out, be like a Sherpa.

Celebrating the Small Victories

The journey into Nepal was an adventurer's dream. After our flight from Kathmandu, we took the week-long trek through the beautiful high countryside and small villages leading to Everest base camp. Worn trails and stone paths led us across rolling hills and sloping valleys, with the Himalayan peaks looking down at us all the while. As we became accustomed to the Central Asian alpine scenery, we learned about its inhabitants as well. The people we met were every bit as proud and captivating as the mountains surrounding them. At every stop, we were greeted with smiling faces and warm hugs. Families who had little to share, heartily invited us into their homes. Everyone we met was eager to help or make a friend, even though they expected nothing in return.

The base camp itself was not unlike the sites we'd been through on other mountains around the world, except everything was bigger. The three-month haul up the mountain required a small army of support, along with tons of gear. In any given season, there might be fifty or more teams trying to make their way up the mountain, each consisting of anywhere from 5 to 25 people. Base camp, sitting at 17,000 feet, is where all those people and their equipment come together in a sprawling collection of tents and piles. There were parties from every corner of the globe. Some were experienced climbers who had saved for a shot at their holy grail. Others were wealthy adventurers who had purchased the best gear and help money could buy in hopes of finding a way to the top. No matter their background, everyone was keenly aware of the excitement and danger that lurked in the weeks ahead. Everest was a place where you could find glory or die trying, and scores of people each climbing season did.

While the mountain is popular with the public and the media, (a simple web search will yield hundreds of books, articles and movies), few people appreciate how difficult it actually is to climb. During the three-month undertaking, you don't just go up once. In fact, through a series of ascents and descents to and from the camps on the route, you actually have to go up and down the lower sections of Everest about 5 times. This is partly to do with your gear. All of the oxygen canisters, coats, ice axes, and other implements required for a shot at the summit must be moved by foot from base camp to the top. This represents literally tons of equipment for each person, and, at the risk of stating the blatantly obvious, moving it uphill through fields of ice at high altitude is no easy task.

More importantly, however, is the need to acclimatize as the body just can't function there without taking some time to adjust. Consider this: If you could be flown by helicopter to the summit of Everest right this second, with all the best equipment to take with you, you'd be unconscious within five minutes, and dead within ten. Not because of the frigid temperatures, rather, it's that the oxygen is so thin your brain would swell in a matter of moments. Even at base camp, which is higher than many of the greatest mountains outside the Himalayas, it's not uncommon to see headaches, vomiting and other effects of altitude sickness. It's only by taking months moving into and out of the camps, inching your way up the mountain, that you can give your body a fighting chance at surviving to see the top.

Beyond the problems of air and altitude, Everest carries the same weather and terrain dangers as any other high-altitude peak. Blizzards, avalanches, and falling rocks kill climbers each year. Assorted illnesses and falls routinely claim victims as well. It's understood when you set off from base camp that the best you can do is look out for the obvious dangers, and then pray that you'll be alright.

In that department, we were open to any help we could get. Nearly every team that passes through base camp stops to see the monks who hold a blessing ceremony for climbers on their way up. We had the good fortune of passing through at a time when a Rinpoche, a high-ranking Buddhist religious figure, was milling about. He was exactly the way you'd picture a monk should be. At about four feet tall with heavily lined dark skin and a heavy accent, he looked like an earthly Yoda in his saffron robes. At our request, he agreed to perform the blessing personally. After we'd all gathered, he offered us what we came to learn were the prerequisites for praying – Russian vodka and Chinese whiskey. Once we had all imbibed, he read from a copy of the Tibetan Book of Prayers that appeared to have predated fire. It had a sort of leather covering and ancient pages held together with a kind of yarn. We arranged ourselves and our climbing gear in a circle around a chorton, a small pile of rocks in the center. For over an hour he rumbled the passages in low tones, more of a chant than a recital, dabbing each of us and our equipment with yak butter.

When he had finished blessing our expedition, he went around to each of us to offer words of good fortune and encouragement. In the dim light from the tent fire, and with nearly two dozen of us in the room, he hadn't realized Erik was blind, and no one had told him. As he placed his hand out to shake hands, Erik felt out in front of him and offered his hand at an angle away from the small monk. The Rinpoche turned to me with a confused look, forced a pained smile, and in his broken English asked, "he also going?"

When we explained about our blind friend, the Rinpoche became quiet. After a moment of contemplating, he asked us each for an empty film canister, which we produced. He disappeared momentarily, and then returned with the canisters. Each had been filled with dried rice he had blessed. He instructed us to take the canisters with us, and toss a pinch of the rice into the wind as an offering any time we felt particularly frightened or endangered. I remember thinking to myself, *we're on Everest, how would I know when that would be?*

Just beyond base camp lies Everest's first major challenge, as well as one of its most deadly. The Khumbu Ice Fall is a large glacier field with huge crevasses cut into its floor that descend thousands of feet down, and sometimes more. A jumbled mess of chaos running about a mile long and sloping upward a few thousand feet, its traps shift daily as glaciers burn and expand under the sun. Passing through is extremely treacherous, a thought that never leaves your mind as the frozen columns groan and crack around you. The only way through is by stepping over a series of aluminum ladders that have been roped together as makeshift bridges to carry you over the dark pits. The Sherpas liked to tell us that if we fell, the crevasses were so deep that we'd end up back in America. I wasn't inclined to doubt them. There are a thousand ways to die in Khumbu; falling is only the most terrifying of them.

Everyone we'd spoken to had stressed the importance of moving through the Ice Fall as quickly as possible, and I could see why. The longer you were there, the bigger the risk that a chunk of ice would break off from one of the surrounding walls and crush you or that the ground would shift and you'd be swallowed by a deep crevasse. Worse still was the psychological effect. Simply put, the Ice Fall terrorized your mind. As I made my way across the first series of ladders, which swayed and moved under my weight, my heart rendered most of my body numb. The only thing keeping me from a freefall into the endless, dark oblivion below were a few discount ladders tied together by some sort of Sherpa Kmart boat twine. A kind of minor panic set in with each step, until I reached the end of a pit, only to feel a moment's relief before facing the next one.

Things were going slowly, but I was making progress. Until I reached the long crevasse bridged by six ladders, that is. One or two had been tolerable, but this was sheer insanity. It stretched on and on, the middle ladders sagging noticeably downward. I told my legs to keep going forward, but my body refused to move. I finally took the first step, only to watch the ladder at the far end jolt and slide. I closed my eyes and tried to regain my calm, taking one small rung at a time under my feet. The flimsy support below me was still gliding right to left as sweat poured down into my eyes. In my fear, I did the worst thing you can ever do in the Ice Fall – I looked down.

What I saw wasn't nothing, it was worse than that. The sheer blackness extended down forever, and it seemed to be drawing me closer. I could feel it wanting to swallow me, like the frozen gateway to an icy hell. There was no sound, no movement or expression, only its unrelenting pull. Paralyzed, I thought of my pinch of rice. Moving slowly so as not to upset the balance below me, I carefully took the film canister from the side pocket where I'd stowed it and dumped every last grain into the pit. We all had a good laugh, and I was able to pull myself together.

Having gotten past my terror, I was able to regain my focus and work my way to the far end and onto solid ice. With each section completed, I had to turn and try to calmly guide Erik across verbally. I had explained to him what we'd be crossing and the dire consequences if he got it wrong. Watching him from a dozen yards away, every step was nerve-racking.

Holding onto ropes for guidance and feeling the edges of the ladders beneath him to make out his steps, Erik made his way over the crevasses. I was surprised at his strong progress, until he came to the middle of a long section and stopped. The ice around us had been groaning from the punishment offered by the afternoon sun. I was worried my friend was suffering from the same brand of terror that I had, and I wanted to comfort him. In the calmest voice I could muster, I asked "Are you scared?"

Erik paused and put on his most thoughtful expression. "I'm fine, but I'm not sure this construction would be in compliance with the Americans with Disabilities Act."

Erik flashed a big grin and I broke out laughing in spite of myself. How could he be making jokes at a time like this? Later, I found out the secret to Erik's quick progress in the Ice Fall. Because he couldn't see, he didn't have the temptation to look down and be distracted by the fear of falling. For him, the ladders were just like any other place on Everest, or any other mountain for that matter. He had to focus and concentrate on each step, or he wouldn't make it. There was no room in his attention for what would come before or after that, only the immediate task in front of him.

Over the next few months, we shuttled through the ice fall more than a dozen times. It was never easy, but I had learned my lesson from Erik's example after that first crossing and it served me well on Everest, and afterward, in life. Taking on any large project, like climbing Mount Everest, can seem overwhelming. The way to get through it is to focus on what's in front of you and celebrate the minor victories. See the big picture, know why you're doing what you're doing, but don't let that keep you from moving forward. The only way to beat a large mountain is with millions of small steps.

Death By Chocolate

Standing next to Everest, and connected to it, is the Lhotse Shar. The world's fourth highest mountain, Lhotse is a mammoth in its own right and would be a major climbing destination in any other setting. As it is, anyone looking to scale Everest via the traditional routes has to spend a significant amount of time making their way across Lhotse in order to make a summit attempt on its taller sister. The mountain's western flank is known as the Lhotse Face. With nearly 4,000 feet of glacial blue ice extending to the South Col of Everest, the Face is an extremely dangerous place to be. Along with the usual dangers of altitude, its heavy slope – ranging from fifty degrees to completely vertical – means that objects like rocks can come falling down at any time.

A few years ago, an experienced climber was making his way up the Lhotse Face. He was doing everything right, not taking any careless chances or pushing himself too hard or too quickly. Reaching his arm up for the next grip, he saw a small dot coming down at him. He wasn't able to get out the way quickly enough and the object hit him in the chest. What he had thought was a small stone had bounced off him and finally come to rest in a pile of snow a few feet below. The object wasn't a stone at all, but a Snickers bar someone had dropped out of their bag from a few-hundred feet above him. Frozen through from the extreme cold, the candy bar had become the equivalent of a brick dropped from 30 or 40 stories above.

The hard thud of the impact seemed to knock the wind out of him. Unable to find his breath, he halted his ascent and waited for help. When his climbing partners reached him, they found him wheezing and struggling to get his words out. By feeling under his jacket and listening to his breath, his teammates were able to figure out that the candy bar had broken two of his ribs, causing one to puncture his lung.

Knowing they would have to act quickly to get help, they decided to evacuate the climber down. By the time he reached camp a few hours later, however, he was losing consciousness. That night, he died.

His story is unfortunate, but not as unusual as you might think. On a mountain, there are a thousand things that can get you at any moment. Falls, weather, and even the occasional rogue snack can do you in. It's dangerous, but I also think it makes climbers fortunate in a way. It makes us realize how fragile life is, and how quickly everything you have can be gone in the blink of an eye. We appreciate our families, our homes, our jobs so much more because we've all come too close to losing them.

I know most people will never climb a huge mountain – they're too smart for that. They might think Everest is a dangerous place, and he had it coming just for being there. They might be right. But don't fool yourself into thinking that things only happen on mountains. Take the time to appreciate your family, your friends, and your life. You never know where your chocolate bar might be falling from.

Winds of Change

On our own journey up the Lhotse Face, Erik and I labored through seven hours of intense exhaustion. Despite our fatigue, however, we were in great spirits. The sky was clear, and we were nearing our attempt on the Everest summit. It was hard to believe our great luck. Lhotse is known for massive storms but we were sneaking through on a clear morning...or so we thought.

About half an hour from the end of the last pitch, I stopped to take a few pictures of the face. Through the camera's view, I could make out a small cloud creeping in from above. It looked to be nothing more than a speck, but I couldn't believe how quickly it was moving. The combination of high alpine terrain, the heavy summer sun and jet-stream force winds at that altitude means that weather or wind might be going over 70 or 80 miles per hour. Aware of how quickly things could change in the Himalayas, I immediately called to Erik to stop what he was doing and brace himself.

Working in a mad scramble, we dug out any protection that we could and roped ourselves into the line. Thirty seconds later, our clear skies had been replaced by a pounding storm. It had taken half a minute to go from a clear day into a heavy alpine blizzard, complete with pounding snow and nearly tornado-force winds. Those few moments were all the warning we received to recognize the changing situation and prepare for it.

As we went on, we learned to recognize and anticipate Everest's mood swings. No matter what you were doing or where you were, you had to be prepared for a tempestuous storm at any time. One of the key elements of success for us, and probably any other team for that matter, was flexibility, the ability to be ready to change and adapt. Directions change, plans change, life changes. Make yourself ready, because the job or the life you have right now probably won't be the same for long. Keep your eye on the ridge, watch for the weather, and be prepared.

Ten Thousand Steps

Babu Chiri Sherpa was the undisputed reigning champ on Everest. Not only had he reached the summit ten times, but he had also set the mind-staggering speed record from base camp to summit in 16 hours. In another display of raw human skill, he'd become the first climber to intentionally spend the night at the top of the mountain, a good 3,000 feet into the death zone.

His success on the mountain had granted him fame in his home country of Nepal, as well as with climbers around the world, so I was excited to get the chance to meet him during our first week at Everest base camp. All the teams had gathered for a kind of orientation dinner as a brief chance to see and meet the parties with whom we'd be sharing the mountain. Two things about this man struck me immediately. The first was that he was genuinely kind and soft-spoken. You'd never have known from his humble, generous attitude that he was a mountaineering celebrity. The second thing I noticed right away was he was fat. He certainly wasn't obese, but it was clear the iron man I'd always pictured as a kind of tenacious bear could put away the groceries.

I didn't see Babu again until several weeks later. Our team was spending the night at Camp II, but I hadn't been feeling well. The weather was good, so I decided to make my way down to base camp to spend a day of rest at the lower elevation regaining some strength. As I made my way through the ice fall, I came upon a pair who were making their way down, but seemed to be struggling.

When I reached them I was able to make out Babu as the first climber. He had a short rope attached to his waist extending only a few feet away to a climber behind him. He seemed to be using the rope's tension, along with verbal commands to guide the second man. They weren't making quick progress. I caught up with them quickly, and Babu explained his predicament.

The second climber, Babu's client, had cerebral edema, an excess of fluid in the brain that can be brought on by altitude sickness. It is not uncommon on Everest, but it can be deadly. Among its many symptoms – headaches, hallucinations, and loss of coordination - the condition can also lead to temporary blindness. This man had lost his sight higher up, and now Babu was trying to help him back down through the ice fall to the safety of base camp.

I couldn't believe the coincidence. In a thousand years, I wouldn't have been able to dream up a situation in which Babu could use my help on Everest. He had forgotten more about mountaineering than I'd ever learn. But here he was, trying to guide a blind man through the Ice Fall, a topic I knew something about.

After quickly explaining this to Babu, we rearranged ourselves to guide the man across the maze of ladders and crevasses that stood between us and safer ground. Using the techniques I'd honed over my years working with Erik, we were able to reach base camp only a couple of hours later. Once we'd arrived, both Babu and his client thanked me profusely. I explained it had been my privilege to help, and then headed to our team's area for some rest.

The next morning, Babu sought me out in my tent, asking if he could show his gratitude more formally by inviting me to his mess tent in base camp for Sherpa tea and cookies. I didn't feel as though any additional thanks were needed, but I wasn't going to pass up the chance to spend a couple of hours with climbing royalty. I cheerfully accepted, and we made our way to his tent.

For two hours, Babu and I traded climbing stories and details of our lives. True to his humble nature, he insisted on calling me "Mr. Jeff," and continually insisted I have more cookies than would be polite for me to accept. As when we'd first met, I was truly in awe of the man, not only because of the spectacular feats he had accomplished in the Himalayas, but also because he managed to hold himself with such grace and integrity. As we parted ways, I tried to impress upon him what an honor it had been to have shared in his time. I walked away beaming, knowing I had a memory I'd always treasure.

Three days later, I got the news that Babu had died. He was settled in with his clients at Camp II, a relatively safe area of the mountain. Like anywhere else on Everest, it has its dangers, but the area was mostly flat, with small, easily avoidable crevasses. As the story went, he decided to step out of his tent at dusk and take a few photos for his family. He had backed himself up a couple of feet to get a wider angle, and slipped into a hole. Babu fell ninety feet, landing on his head and dying instantly.

I was shocked by the news, as was his country. Babu was more than a climbing icon; he was a great man in every sense of the word. It seemed impossible he could have been killed in a safer area of the mountain on a clear day, but that is the nature of mountaineering, and the way of life. No matter who you are and what you've done, you can never decide you're going to take it easy. Those moments in our lives and careers when we think we've got it made are often the most deadly, when our confidence can do away with us. I learned two great things from Babu: that a great man can be humble, and that, even after 10,000 right steps, you can't afford a wrong one.

Good Times at Eight Thousand Meters

In the months after we'd made our first trip through the ice fall, we continued our slow crawl up Everest, moving ourselves and our gear from camp to camp up the mountain and back down again. The repeated hauls from base camp wore on endlessly until our arrival at Camp III weeks later, but they would prepare our bodies and equipment for a summit assault.

Camp III itself was little more than a semi-flat area carved out on the side of a glacier. Blustery and freezing at over 24,000 feet, it was a miserable place to sleep. There's nothing but ice below you, and the wind rips at you viciously through the night. Worst of all, however, was the snow drifting down the side of the mountain. As strong gusts whipped the tent, small pockets of powder would fill in beneath the floor, tilting it up and threatening to slide us off a cliff and into oblivion.

Luckily, we only spent one sleepless night before moving on. When early morning arrived, we were all anxious to leave behind Camp III and its nightmarish elements for the real dangers higher up. With every increase in elevation, the altitude becomes more and more treacherous. Out of the hundreds of people who have died on the mountain, most have been at the top tiers. High winds clear the snow, leaving only ice and loose rocks for footing. It's easier to slip and fall, and the consequences for doing so are more severe. To make matters worse, your oxygen-starved brain starts making bad decisions. In a place where you can't afford a single mental error, you're reduced to the brainpower of a yak by the lack of air.

To somewhat mitigate this, we began taking oxygen from canisters, coming out of Camp III. They didn't restore our air to what it would be like at sea level, but they did give us that extra bit of breathable gas that could make the difference. Among Everest fanatics, there has been a long debate of whether using supplemental oxygen on the mountain is sporting. The first groups to summit in the fifties used oxygen, as do most modern teams. Still, there are some groups of climbers who consider using oxygen to be 'cheating.' Mountaineers, they feel, should rely on their own physical assets to make their ascents, and nothing more. Our team had discussed this, but we agreed almost immediately we wanted to use every tool we had at our disposal to increase our chances of success. For me, it was never an issue. I wouldn't think of going up Everest without oxygen, any more than I would think about climbing it barefoot. The air was a valuable tool that helped me stay alive, and I was glad for it.

Shortly out of camp, we moved up across angular, rocky growth called the Yellow Band and another called the Geneva Spur. It was a long day of climbing, but even in my exhaustion I couldn't help but marvel at the beauty of it. They weren't the kinds of spectacular views you'd see on a postcard, but the simple fact that they were so close to the highest summit on earth made them captivating. As the day wore on, I tried to savor the experience and take in everything I could before we finally settled in for the evening. It occurred to me that I might never see these places again after we left the mountain. But my thoughts turned as we reached our destination for the day. Things were serious now – Camp IV and the eight-thousand meter death zone.

The death zone isn't a mysterious or dramatic climbing name; it's a simple reminder of where you are. At 8,000 meters, or about 26,000 feet, the human body has a hard time finding or extracting oxygen from the atmosphere. At one-third the air pressure you'd find at sea level, there just isn't enough of it to go around. As a result, lots of bad things start to happen. Obviously, it gets hard to breath. Climbing uphill feels like you're running a marathon while breathing through a straw. Vomiting and diarrhea are normal occurrences. Sleep is hard to find, where pounding headaches are not. Typically, a person won't feel hungry or thirsty, which is just as well because the stomach can't absorb any nutrition from the food so it just goes right through you. The body does still need protein, however, so it begins to breakdown muscle tissue in an effort to cannibalize itself. Topping it off is an extreme cold, even by alpine standards. Any piece of exposed skin will pick up frostbite. Hands and feet are vulnerable as well, meaning that even those who make the summit often pay with missing fingers and toes. In short, at 8,000 meters you're dying quickly, and the only thing you can do to stop it is leave.

We arrived at Camp IV in the afternoon, with the intention of leaving for the summit at night. If the weather cooperated, we'd climb through the evening and arrive at the summit just after daybreak. However, when the whole team had finally arrived and gotten settled, it became obvious we weren't all going to be ready. A few of us could probably have made a successful attempt, but as a whole, the group was too tired and ragged. We'd come all that way and we had to make a difficult choice: either some of us could push through and try to summit, or we could risk taking a night at Camp IV and hope that all, or any, of us could make it with an extra day's rest.

It was late May, near the end of climbing season. In a few days, the Sherpas below would pull down the ladders that made traversing the Ice Fall possible, meaning a return to Camp IV would not be possible. And even if it were, we didn't have the supplies or the strength for another go at it. There was only going to be one shot. After all the time training and preparing, tens of thousands of dollars spent, and 10 weeks on the mountain, I expected a heated argument between those who felt they could make it and those who were too exhausted. To my surprise, however, there was no conflict. After we'd gotten into our tents and opened the conversation via radio, we went around one by one to determine each climber's readiness. It quickly became apparent we couldn't all go on, so the team decided to stay another day, with no discussion of splitting up or leaving anyone behind. If we could make it after a night in the death zone, that would be wonderful. If we couldn't, then we'd be able to say we came and left as a team.

For twenty-four hours, we milled around, trying to save whatever strength we could while our bodies ate at themselves. We passed the time by trying to sleep and or play cards in our tents. Even with a Braille deck, it's normally not that difficult to beat Erik at a game of poker. Usually a slight lean is all it takes to figure out if he's bluffing or not. With oxygen masks on, however, my cheating was accompanied by a Darth Vader sound effect. Again and again, I'd maneuver for a closer look, only to find my snooping met with a hard punch to the chest. As we played, blustery storms slapped at the sides of our tent. It sounded as if the world was going to hell outside our nylon walls, but we tried to keep it out of our minds.

I woke on the second night, minutes before the alarm was set to go off. It was pitch black, and there was no sound except the wind slapping away at the walls of our tent. Slowly, I sat up and turned on my headlamp. One by one, my teammates did the same. We began waking ourselves and getting equipment in order, but no one spoke. Our small tent was like a locker room on Super bowl Sunday. We were in for the biggest day of our climbing lives and we all knew it. Except for a few nearly-hidden smirks, no one wanted to acknowledge or jinx the moment.

In the near darkness, we set about the work of getting our packs together. We knew we'd be away from camp for at least twenty-four hours, moving to even higher and more dangerous ground. We had to be absolutely sure we had anything and everything we might need, and knew where to find it. We packed and checked again and again, knowing anything forgotten might cost a life.

With everything we hoped to need stowed into place, we stepped outside the tent and into the wind tunnel outside. We gathered together for one last count, and any final thoughts or instructions. After some of the team gave a few thoughts on the weather and some notes of encouragement, Erik stepped forward. I thought he was going to offer profound words of wisdom, or perhaps say something motivational to the team, but instead he did something better... he pulled aside his oxygen mask and puked.

Some people might have considered this to be a bad omen, especially at that altitude, but I was elated. Over the years, I'd come to see Erik's vomit as a sign of good fortune to come. On every major mountain we'd gone up together - Denali, Aconcagua, Rainier, and others - a successful summit had been preceded by my blind friend emptying his stomach. I never knew why he did it, but I knew what it meant. It was time to get him to the top.

Dig It

We filed out one by one into the darkness, leaving Camp IV behind. The sense of anticipation and nervousness that had been with us as we made our preparations soon melted into the hours of trudging up steep snow slopes and across rocky bulges. The wind beat down on us, but we moved efficiently, following each step with a few resting breaths. The object was to keep making progress upward through the packed snow and ice surface below ,while holding on to enough strength to see the night through.

Even though our whole team was in a line moving upward, the setting was intensely isolating. The only thing I could see was the small pocket of light immediately in front of me provided by my headlamp, past that it seemed like the rest of the world had gone away. I found myself lost in my own thoughts, Erik trudging along happily behind me in some of his favorite terrain.

It was as we were packing our equipment that I first noticed a strong sensation in my chest. It was hardly noticeable at first, but as we made our final preparations and set off into the cold night, it grew stronger. It wasn't a pain, but a tingle that was welling up inside me. With my medical training, I knew the cardiovascular risks we'd taken by being at altitude so long, but I didn't feel afraid. The sensation wasn't hurting me, it felt more like it was giving me strength. Now, making our way over the ice bulge, I could feel it increasing. The farther we buried ourselves into the thick, stormy night, the better I felt.

Instead of fading down, the storm that had accompanied us since we woke seemed to be picking up strength. We could hear thunder through the roaring wind, and we weren't sure how much further we'd be able to keep going. Lightning is a very rare event on Everest, but with climbing gear and metal oxygen tanks strapped to our bodies, it wasn't something to take lightly. As the rough weather drew nearer, we kept an ongoing discussion on our radios, eventually deciding to go just a little farther and see if it would fizzle out.

Despite our worries about the weather, I found myself continuing to feel better and stronger. The sensation in my chest was driving me on, and my pace started to pick up. Chris and Erik, who were immediately behind me, urged me to forge on ahead, so I let my legs go free and started passing some of my team members. Eventually I found myself at the front of the group and decided to venture out ahead a couple dozen yards.

I recognized a rock feature that would mark our halfway point to the summit. We had agreed we should stop there to assess whether we'd be able to continue. The thunderstorm we feared was still raging in the distance, but things seemed to be going very well otherwise. Despite the fact that we'd spent an extra day at Camp IV in the death zone, we were in a groove. Everyone was moving along at a brisk pace. I stopped to look ahead. Behind the electric flashes, a small dot of light was peeking through. As I waited for the rest of the group to arrive, it grew larger and brighter, until I could make out the outline of perhaps the most beautiful thing I've ever seen. The sun was rising just over the Everest summit, casting an inviting glow over the mountain. I spent a few awestricken minutes, taking it in before I turned to face my team. We all nodded to each other and, without a word, went on.

The feeling in my chest was like a small fire now, driving me farther ahead. My strides came quickly and easily, outpacing those of my teammates. Under the glow of the sun, I was free to wander farther ahead and remain roped in and within site. As I pushed higher, the storm that had threatened to engulf us had fallen just short. It was sitting a few dozen yards below our feet, spread out like a carpet under the ridge we were working up. The clouds were nearly perfectly flat, the lightning popping like squares on a disco floor. It was spectacular, but I wondered if my brain was suffering from oxygen deficiency. As a medical professional and someone who's seen 107 Grateful Dead shows, I know that not everything your mind conjures up under those conditions exists in the outside world. But, to my relief, my teammates were amazed at the same awesome sight. For those few minutes, we walked on the clouds.

All through the night, we'd been following a set of ropes left by a previous team who had chosen the same route. We didn't need them necessarily to find the way, but they would be critical for the descent if a storm were to move in and disorient us. At that altitude, a nice 80 mile-an-hour gust could push a climber directly off the side of the mountain and into a half-mile fall. Likewise, we could use them on the way back down from the summit. In white-out conditions, a climber could lose his orientation and step right off the side of a cliff, as one had done the previous day.

I'd reached a point, however, where the ropes stopped. We were about a quarter of a mile from the south summit, a peak just a few hundred vertical feet and a couple of hours from the actual summit. The way forward was obvious, but the ropes were buried under a couple feet of snow. A new rope had been fixed, veering off onto a different path 40 feet to the left that led through a field of rocky shale.

I had come to what I call my leadership moment. It was my chance to choose the easy way, or to sacrifice for my team. I had been feeling great, and the short detour on the left would have given me a fairly quick trip up to the south summit, with the final summit just a short journey beyond. The sun had come out and burned away the clouds, leaving us with a clear, windless morning. This would be the best chance I could ever hope for to achieve every climber's dream, reaching the top of the highest mountain. But I knew from my years of guiding Erik that the detour route would be very difficult for him. The ground was almost completely loose shale. It would be like walking on broken dish plates, taking a few steps forward not only to get ahead, but to fight the tendency to slide backward. That kind of ground was exhausting for him, and I knew he might not be able to navigate it and still have the strength to push for the summit.

The way ahead would be great going for him, but it would mean digging out the ropes. In the thin mountain air, the effort would be excruciating. It would mean more than an hour of work, and I'd certainly be too exhausted to go on afterward. I finally understood what that feeling in my chest was, and what it was for. I took one more look to my left and the easy path. I followed it with my eyes up the south summit, through the small ridge beyond, and up to the goal that had been a dream for so many years. Then, I took a deep breath and let it go. It was time to dig.

I was surprised to find that I wasn't bothered by my decision. I'd come to Everest to help Erik get to the top, my aspirations were secondary. I had done my job and would probably make it to the south summit. It wasn't the summit, but it was close, and I didn't need to take it any farther than that. I think it was in that moment I finally understood what leadership is all about. It's not defined by a title or a role, or how many people answer to you. It's about seeking opportunities to step up and showing your team you're willing to put their success above your own. These chances come every day, whether working on a mountain or in a cubicle, you just have to take them.

With the decision made, I started to chop into the ice and pull the ropes free. It was tedious and tiring, but also comforting to know my long trip was near an end. I knew with certainty I would not be able to continue on. My arms burned from the effort, and my lungs screamed as I drove my ice axe down again and again, freeing a few inches of rope with each blow. Finally, I neared the end of the digging as the team caught up from behind. As the first climbers came within a few yards, I broke the last block of ice, springing the rope up in a taught line to the south summit. The work was finished, and so was I. I could barely breath, and even the sensation in my chest that had given me such a deep well of strength was exhausted.

I fell down to my knees. I looked back to my climbing partners and a huge wave of satisfaction rolled over me. One by one, they came to me as they realized what had happened, and offered their thanks. Erik had been last on the line and was the final teammate to reach me. He asked if I could go on, although he had to have known I was depleted. Looking across the ridge, I knew I couldn't make it. It was possible I'd reach the top, but I'd never have the strength to get back down. Beneath my mask, I tried to force a smile. "Tagging the summit is optional," I answered, "but going home isn't." Neither of us spoke for a moment. After everything we'd gone through together, it was finally time to reach the highest point, and I'd given it up for him.

Erik looked back to me. "Can you get down?" he asked, the pain evident in his voice. I told him I could. He seemed to be trying to undo the moment, not wanting to accept the situation.

And then, my friend did the only thing he could: he thanked me, gave me a hug, and went to finish his ascent.

I sat on my knees watching Chris and Erik catch up with the rest of the group at the south summit. From there, it would be a two hour climb across a daunting ridge, followed by a short climb to the top. I couldn't believe he was actually going to do it. After all the experts and critics had told us why it would be impossible, he was going to beat this thing. I was in no hurry to make my way down, just taking in the calm and quiet of the setting. The summit pyramid seemed so close I could touch it, sitting like a jewel with the moon hanging just above it. From so near the top, I could see the deep shadow it cast over Nepal, holding miles and miles in darkness hours after daybreak. I wondered if Everest would cast a shadow in my life as well, knowing I'd made it so close to the top without succeeding.

As I pondered this, the group reached the south summit. Erik turned back one last time to wave in my direction, and then continued on. I knew he was going to reach the top, and I wanted more than anything to share that moment with him. At the risk of sounding mystical, I feel that life gives you a nudge sometimes. I've always tried to keep watch for those times when the world seems to be speaking to me, and this was one of them. After sitting in resignation for nearly 5 minutes, some of my strength had returned. I didn't know if it was enough for me to make it, but I didn't want to spend the rest of my life wondering. With my last bit of strength, I rose to meet and followed behind.

Beyond the south summit, you follow a ridge towards the top that becomes very steep very quickly. One wrong step to the right wins you a 10,000 foot drop into Tibet, while the prize for slipping to the left is a 6,000 foot fall into Nepal. If I fell, I was convinced it was probably going to hurt pretty badly. I thought of this as I tried to settle my rubbery legs and make my way through. It only took about an hour to catch up to the rest of the group. I fell in behind Erik and Chris. If there were any questions about why I'd changed my mind, my teammates kept them to themselves. We were all too exhausted to have the conversation.

Past the ridge lay the Hillary Step, the most famous 40 feet of climbing granite in the world. When Sir Edmund and his team first scaled the mountain in 1953, the Englishman relied on aerial reconnaissance to map out routes to the top. The photos available at the time had masked the short rock face that serves as the last barrier to the summit. With no way around it, he simply powered his way over it to reach the top. The face has borne his name ever since.

I had always thought if I reached the Step, I would climb it gracefully. I wanted to approach it like a work of art, a sort of climbing ballet. In reality, by the time I arrived, my body felt beat up and ruined. Unable to muster any technique or finesse, I embarked upon the ugliest piece of climbing you've ever seen. I flopped my arms upward, like a fish on the deck of a boat, hoping my hand would find some grip. Slowly and painfully, I heaved and convulsed my way up over the granite face in grotesque exhibition. I think I even tried to use Erik's foot as a hold a couple of times. In the end it didn't matter, because 30 minutes later I was standing on top of the world with a blind man.

The View From the Top

The summit of Mount Everest was unbelievable, but not for the reasons you'd think. It's not the being there that made it special, but the getting there. The place itself is a small flat area, no more than three feet by three feet. As you're walking up the last ridge you simply reach a point where you can't go any higher or farther – you're at the highest point on Earth. Erik and I hugged, and we each shed a few tears that froze to our cheeks. We both knew we'd taken the long route to the top.

A lot of climbers say they go up big mountains to take in the spectacular views from top. I think these people are selling themselves short. Erik would be the first to tell you the view from any summit is overrated, and while I doubt his credentials for making that claim, I agree with him wholeheartedly. The view is incredible, but it isn't worth what we went through for almost three months to get there, and it certainly isn't worth risking your life in the death zone to see. The only thing that makes Everest, or any adventure worth it, is the chance to challenge yourself and take in the experience.

I'm often asked what I thought about on the summit. For

the longest time, I tried to think of a profound answer to that question. I wanted to tell people that a life-changing secret was bestowed upon me by the climbing gods, or that I felt some deep wisdom fill me. Sadly, that's not the case. The reality is, after I'd taken a moment to celebrate and posed for a few photos, the only thought that came to me was, "Now, how in the hell am I going to get down?"

You see, when you get to the summit, you're only halfway. You've gotten all the way up the mountain, but you still have to get all the way down, which is often the hardest part. Three-quarters of all mountaineering accidents happen *after* the ascent. It isn't that the terrain is any tougher than before, it's because human nature sets in. People are exhausted and become complacent. They've already done what they came to do, so they lose focus and stop watching their feet. It's not unusual for a climber to make a major assault on a technically difficult summit and then walk off a cliff, get caught in a storm, or simply fall and slide off the side of a ridge. People think enlightenment comes to you at the top of a mountain, but it's actually the one place on a mountain where you don't learn very much.

Most of us are given a handful of summits in our lives, and usually we think of these 'big days' as those that define us. Weddings, promotions, children's births and other completed adventures make easy landmarks by which we judge everything else. Nevertheless, it's important to remember that while we celebrate at the summit, the rest of life takes place on the side of the mountain. The challenge is to recognize that, and find a way to understand it and apply it to our lives. It's all those days moving up and down, all of those small challenges, that make us who we are. Without them, the summit wouldn't mean anything. The real joy in your life can be found in the challenges, not the achievements.

Teamwork: From Boardrooms to Base Camp

S ince that summer on Everest, hundreds of groups around the world have hired me to talk about teamwork. The parallels between working together on a mountain and the kind of cooperation it takes to succeed in business or any other endeavor are obvious, and I've loved having the chance to share the lessons of my life with others. None of the accomplishments Erik and I have tasted would have been possible if we weren't able to rely on each other and our other teammates. Most people realize this and expect me to speak about the other climbers who were with us on our expeditions, but I let them know that our support ran so much deeper than that.

In planning for Everest, I really started to get a feel for exactly how large our team had to be. The whole thing was such a massive undertaking that we simply couldn't handle everything ourselves. There was no way to get our arms around it. At first, we sought out other climbers who would be interested in helping us make the ascent. More than a dozen men and women came forward to help us achieve the impossible, even though they knew the risks to us and themselves. From there, we had to seek out Sherpa support staff in the Himalayas. As I've mentioned, these are some of the hardest working guys on earth. There is never any shortage of groups wanting to scale Everest, and the best Sherpas can pick and choose who to work with. Once again, through letters, phone calls, and e-mails, we were able to find a group of dedicated individuals who believed in what we were trying to do and wanted to be a part of it.

The climbers and Sherpas who would accompany us on the mountain were only the beginning. We also leaned heavily on our friends and families for emotional support. It's hard to hear dozens of people announce publicly that they expect you to fail, or worse, die. Without the encouragement we got from our families at so many junctures – people like Erik's dad and his brothers, my mother, father and grandparents – the weight of it all might have caused us to abandon our ideas and go for something more 'reasonable.' But with our loved ones behind us, we found the strength to do the extraordinary.

Outside our own circles, so many organizations stepped in. Dozens of mountaineering equipment companies donated gear to help keep us safer than we would have been in very dangerous environments. Magazines and news services gave us coverage that led to hundreds of daily letters and e-mails from readers that helped motivate us to keep trying.

None of our big mountain ascents would have been possible without sponsors who came forward with money and manpower, especially the National Federation For The Blind. When we first floated the idea of climbing Everest to different people, they immediately stepped up and indicated they wanted to help. The risks they took in supporting us were huge. Besides the financial outlay which covered the bulk of our journey and supplies, they stood to face possible backlash from a public relations nightmare if we weren't successful. If we had failed to make any progress, or if something had happened to Erik, they would have had a ton of explaining to do. Their members and supporters would have demanded to know why they'd financed and encouraged a project that seemed bound to fail from the start.

Nevertheless, they decided over what were probably some very heated discussions, to put their marbles in our corner, and once they'd rolled the dice, they gave their full support. The NFB committed everything they had: their money, their time, and their very credibility. They believed in us, even when there wasn't a lot of reason to. They were keenly aware of the risks to their jobs and our lives, but they decided supporting us was the right thing to do.

In the end, it couldn't have turned out any better for the NFB and the other groups that backed us. We made a record-breaking summit of the world's highest peak, garnering global media attention and turning the spotlight to their causes, which never would have happened if they hadn't gambled everything on us to start with.

What I learned from their support was how important it was for us to be connected. Just as on the mountain, we knew our teammates had the confidence in us to believe we'd all succeed or suffer the same fate. Having so many people on our side gave us strength and confidence. It created an environment where we all wanted to succeed for each other, and that made our team much stronger than the individuals who made it up – from Erik and I on the mountain, to the fundraisers and logistical support staff that did all the work behind the scenes. Each of them brought different talents and skills, but more importantly, they were willing to share in our vision.

Whatever your goals might be in life, try to build a strong team for yourself and others. For any of us to be successful, it takes the help of so many others. I live in Boulder, Colorado, a community packed with people who love the outdoors. I know that I'm not even the best climber on my block. But I've reached magnificent summits all over the world because of the help I've gotten from the people around me. As you think about what you'd like to do, remember that you'll need help, too. It's the people in your home, your department at work, your church, or your school who can help you put together the pieces for your summit push, wherever that may be.

Generosity: The Gift of the Summit

I've been very fortunate in this world by having the opportunity to make a living doing what I love, and more. It would have been more than enough for me if I'd been able to find a way to be near the mountains. Instead, I've gotten to scale peaks around the world, make friends in dozens of countries, and get public recognition for my successes. The notoriety that Erik and I gained has even given me the platform to pass along the lessons I've learned through speeches, and now this book.

Recognizing all climbing has given me, I feel like it's my responsibility to give some of it back. I can remember clearly my first taste of sharing my success with others. It was a couple of years after our Everest summit, and Erik and I received a letter from Sabriya Tenberken, a fascinating woman who had gone blind when she was younger. She had wanted to join the German equivalent of the Peace Corps. However, with her condition, the organization rejected her application, too afraid to send her around the world and into harm's way.

Most people would have given up, but she was determined to help those less fortunate. She proceeded with a partner to Tibet, where she formed a school called Braille Without Borders. While blindness is a tough handicap to overcome anywhere, in Tibet it is particularly stark. Beyond the already low incomes and standards that prevail for all children in the country, the blind are stigmatized. It is not uncommon for parents and villagers to believe that children who have lost their site are being punished for harsh crimes in former lives. As a result, they receive substandard care. Many receive no education at all, left to beg in city streets.

Through her school, Braille Without Borders, Sabriya has devoted years to rescuing these children, educating them, and giving them a chance at a new life. And despite a long list of fantastic successes, she's always looking for ways to do more. In that spirit, she wrote to us to see if we would be interested in taking a group of her kids climbing on a local mountain. Erik committed immediately, as did I. It sounded like an opportunity to do something remarkable and have a good time.

To call the experience rewarding or satisfying would be a gross understatement. In the weeks we spent in Tibet, those children taught us more about courage and perseverance than we'd ever learn on a rock face or a glacier. Day after day, they pushed themselves to learn new climbing techniques, overcoming pain and exhaustion not for the glory of reaching any summit, but for the joy of learning something new.

I came away from the experience feeling changed and inspired. I started to seek out more ways to help. One of the organizations I became affiliated with was Global Explorers, a group committed to sharing a love of adventure with young people (www.globalexplorers.org) They organize trips around the world, often giving disadvantaged youths a chance to see places they'd never be able to reach otherwise.

Once or twice a year, I help them put together a trip. Sometimes the destinations are close by. Other times, they're as far away as Peru or Africa. The activities vary as well, from simple hikes to short climbs. The point isn't to make the kids into hard core climbers, it's to empower them to be stronger people. Often, it's their first taste of success, as those first mountains had been to me, that they can take and build upon. No matter where we go, I never come away feeling anything less than utter gratitude for having been a part of it. Helping to pass along my love of adventure to the next generation is a different kind of joy, one that I couldn't reach on my own.

We are all indebted, to some degree or another. Whether it was the parent who sacrificed to give you the best they could, the teacher who went far beyond their job requirements, or the mentor who saw a passion in you, every one of us has been helped along the way. Find a way to keep yourself connected. It isn't just about doing the right thing, find a way you can help someone with your expertise and I guarantee you'll find you're enjoying yourself.

It's been an honor to be able to share my story with so many people. My experiences in the mountains have given me a life beyond my wildest dreams. I hope the things I've learned along the way can help you in your journey as well. Now it's your turn. Find your summit, and when you do, don't forget to share.

Jeff Evans is a mountain guide, professional speaker, and physician assistant. His expeditions have taken him around the world, from the jungles of Africa to the wilds of Alaska, and even to the summit of Mount Everest, where he guided Erik Weihenmayer the first blind climber to reach the top of the world's highest peak. Jeff is the founder and owner of MountainVision Expeditions, a Colorado based adventure guide service, taking clients to some of the most exciting and remote corners of the globe.

Jeff also addresses hundreds of corporate and civic groups around the world every year, weaving his tales of adventure into useful themes and messages for his audience members.

Jeff lives in Boulder, Colorado with his wife Merry Beth and son Jace.

To find out more about Jeff, his keynote presentations, or his guided trips, visit:

www.mountain-vision.com

To order additional copies of this book,
or to inquire about bulk pricing, please contact MountainVision
Books at 303-880-8707
or info@mountain-vision.ocm

Breinigsville, PA USA
09 November 2009
227205BV00001B/6/A